ADULT CIVIC EDUCATION

ADULT CIVIC EDUCATION

By

DAVID L. BOGGS, Ph.D.

Associate Professor of Adult Education
The Ohio State University
Columbus, Ohio

With a Foreword by

William D. Dowling, Ph.D.

CHARLES C THOMAS • PUBLISHER
Springfield • Illinois • U.S.A.

Published and Distributed Throughout the World by

CHARLES C THOMAS • PUBLISHER
2600 South First Street
Springfield, Illinois 62794-9265

© *1991 by* CHARLES C THOMAS • PUBLISHER
ISBN 0-398-05724-9
Library of Congress Catalog Card Number: 90-19190

With THOMAS BOOKS *careful attention is given to all details of manufacturing
and design. It is the Publisher's desire to present books that are satisfactory as to
their physical qualities and artistic possibilities and appropriate for their particular
use.* THOMAS BOOKS *will be true to those laws of quality that assure a good
name and good will.*

Printed in the United States of America
SC-R-3

Library of Congress Cataloging-in-Publication Data

Boggs, David L.
    Adult civic education / by David L. Boggs ; with a foreword by
William D. Dowling.
      p. cm.
    Includes bibliographical references and index.
    ISBN 0-398-05724-9
    1. Adult education—United States.   2. Civics—Study and teaching—
United States.   I. Title.
LC5219.B53   1991
320.4'071'5—dc20
                                              90-19190
                                                 CIP

To Lucy, John, and Jason

FOREWORD

There was a time in the history of adult education in the United States when civic education for adults occupied a more important place than it apparently does as the twentieth century draws to a close. This recollection prompted me to think about two factors while writing this Foreword. First, the need for adult civic education as reflected in the environment in which public decisions are made has most likely never been greater. Second, the thoroughness and calmness of the author's approach to the task of writing about not only the need for adult civic education, but also how educators can do a better job of it.

The first concern led me to a cynicism bordering on pessimism that was too negative, to say the least. That is not a very nice note to sound in a Foreword which should be upbeat, tell the reader a little about what might be encountered in the book, and perhaps a little about precursor conditions which make the book timely, or better yet, timeless.

I thought about civic education for the young and how we probably expect too much from it. I thought about teachable moments adults supposedly have and how adult education misses many of them. I thought about the increasing vocationalism of adult education in the United States and how we seem to help adults learn more and more about less and less. I thought about the inability of public adult education agencies to sponsor debate or even educational adventures that would take their learners beyond the status quo. I thought about the reluctance of adult educators to run the risk of alienating anyone for fear of disrupting campaigns to maintain adequate public school tax levies and higher education budgets from legislatures. And in thinking these thoughts I became downhearted, not because the problems are insurmountable, but because there seemed to be so little adult education literature available in these areas. Adult educators seem at this time, and perhaps in other times as well, to be afflicted with the same short-range syndrome that has infected American business and industry—the future is today and possibly tomorrow, but not the day after.

Fortunately, David Boggs has taken the longer range view that has enabled him to write a book addressing many of these problems. He has done so with hope that is grounded not only in intellectual interest in education for civic competence throughout his career, but also in involvement as an elected public official where he, indeed, can and does make a difference. He brings an academic and practical-in-the-world background to this effort which I believe is reflected in his premises, his arguments, and his recommendations for the practice of adult civic education.

What do I hope the author will have accomplished by writing this book? First, I hope it will be widely read by educators of adults and from it they will develop a rationale and methodology enabling them to reclaim their responsibility to offer multiple opportunities for the civic education of adults. Second, I hope these educators of adults and the chief administrators of the institutions within which they work will take heart and courage from what is written here to withstand the efforts of narrowly-oriented groups who would deny all of us the civic dialogue and disputation that should be an integral part of public life. Third, I hope adult education practitioners and theoreticians will move from the reactive stance I perceive they have adopted to a more professional proactive mode in which they themselves think about public issues and assist their publics to do the same.

This book could turn adult education from being an educational enterprise that focuses an undue amount of attention on excessively individualistic and professional issues to one that has more balance, more influence on communities and the issues they face. Our concern as adult educators should include but transcend making a living and be equally concerned with living a life. An important part of living that life is in the civic realm. Boggs has provided an important document to help educators to help all adults live their lives most advantageously.

William D. Dowling, Ph.D.
Professor of Adult Education
The Ohio State University
Columbus, Ohio

PREFACE

This book is unique in two respects. First, there is no other treatise in modern adult education literature devoted exclusively to the imperative of adult civic education. Second, its tone reflects an intent to be, at times, overtly polemical and reformist concerning the meaning and practice of adult civic education. Civic education prepares learners to function effectively as citizens, and the essence of citizenship lies within the meaning of democracy. Democracy, however, is itself a hybrid of conflicting assumptions about appropriate civic behavior. Since education reflects these assumptions it has been necessary to take issue with many of them and to consider their implications for adult civic education.

Unashamedly, the book presents an ideal of citizenship and the education that is required for it to be realized. All ideals challenge and stretch the boundaries of existing thought and practice. In this sense, the book shares purposes in common with democracy itself. The challenge to democracy is to be truly deliberative, to foster healthy participation of citizens who make choices and give direction to government as the instrument of their choices. The challenge of the book is to: (1) describe the meaning and forms of adult civic education in the context of a scholarly-based conception of citizenship and modern democracy, (2) examine the promise of purposeful adult civic learning activities sponsored by Adult Education agencies for participation in the democratic process, and (3) explore the rich perspectives for understanding the office of citizen available through adult education in the humanities.

Two premises guide this undertaking. First, that citizenship is a dynamic concept, undergoing extensive modification from its Graeco-Roman origins, to our founding Fathers, to the twenty-first century when it will again need to be reformulated to take account of the dramatically changed world situation. Second, that whatever civic education is provided in the formal educational system, it is insufficient to sustain a person for life-long engagement in democracy. Neither newly emerging nor well-established democracies can entrust to schools the sole responsibility for education in the lifelong and evolving phenomenon of citizenship. Of necessity, the civic learning that occurs in schools must be supplemented by those institutions and organizations, public and private, avowedly educational or only incidentally so, which in free societies assume some responsibility for the education of adults.

The contribution every adult can make to public life beyond the voting booth involves continuing to learn the knowledge and skills required of autonomous citizens. Adult Education agencies have by and large failed to help adults acquire this learning. This book considers why this is so and what can be done to help adult educators reclaim, refurbish, and assume their rightful responsibility for adult civic education.

The author is grateful to several people for their assistance with this project. William Dowling has generously and cheerfully borne the brunt of teaching and advising graduate students in adult education at The Ohio State University during the author's absence while writing this book. He has also meticulously read, critiqued, and edited the many drafts that were involved in producing it. I am grateful for his support and guidance, not only during this year, but throughout the time that we have been colleagues in adult education. He, of course, shares no responsibility for the book's shortcomings. Also providing special assistance were two other Ohio State University colleagues—Gilbert Jarvis, Chairperson of the author's academic Department of Educational Studies, and J. Lance Kramer, Assistant Provost for Continuing Education—who made it possible for the author to be relieved of most academic responsibilities and have the time to write this book. Their kindness and encouragement have been instrumental in its completion.

David L. Boggs

CONTENTS

xi

ADULT CIVIC EDUCATION

Chapter 1

INTRODUCTION

Man is a political animal . . . participation
in political decisions is necessary to his fulfillment
and happiness . . . all men can and must be sufficiently
educated and informed to take part in making these decisions
. . . a society must make positive provisions for its development
into a community learning together; for this is what political
participation, government by consent, and the civilization of
the dialogue all add up to.

Robert Maynard Hutchins
American Educator
1959

The purpose of this book is to present and defend the proposition that *citizenship* is the fundamental social imperative for adult education in a free society. That is to say, the primal contribution of adult education in a democracy, before all other purposes it serves, is civic education. Certainly other imperatives stemming from economic and social forces, technological and social change, and demographic and occupational trends should command the attention of adult educators. Yet none of these supersedes the importance of insuring that adults have the competence and disposition to attend to the public's business with all its conflicts, problems, opportunities, and choices.

Democracy is the people's business. While it includes government, government is but one instrument that people can employ to achieve their public ends. Public business includes common purposes and political values, in the sense of the conditions and requirements that citizens expect and are willing to work to achieve in their communities and in the larger world. Examples include the activities of citizens to achieve and maintain safe streets, clean air, adequate health care, quality education, parks, public transit, preservation of endangered species, elimination of apartheid, and a community infrastructure of service and philanthropic organizations.

All the purposes adults seek to attain through additional education—such as economic and professional advancement, personal enrichment, literacy, occupational competence, and the like—in the end rest upon democracy as an enabling condition. None of the imperatives to which Adult Education agencies respond is immune to the debilitating consequences of erosion of a strong and active sense of citizenship. The very essence of democracy rests on a self-governing community of citizens who, according to well-known proponent of participatory democracy Benjamin Barber (1984), "are united less by homogeneous interests than by civic education and who are made capable of common purpose and mutual action by virtue of their civic attitudes and participatory institutions rather than their altruism or their good nature" (p. 117).

Ensuring citizen understanding of rights and obligations toward the well-being of society has to be a major educational concern. Since democracy is the context and the condition for everything else that is valued—work, family life, religion, politics, recreation, and leisure—preserving its vitality and integrity has to be a central objective of Adult Education agencies. Other educational purposes presuppose the fertile soil of a flourishing democracy and emanate from it as spokes from the hub of a wheel. By insisting that citizens be instructed in their obligations for the greater common good, society insures the conditions for individual and group objectives to be fulfilled as well.

The question is how to infuse an understanding of citizen responsibilities in educational programs for learners as diverse as pharmacists (Continuing Professional Education), tradesmen (Adult Vocational Education), and high school drop-outs (Adult Basic Education)? For example, the focus of continuing professional education is the changing knowledge and competence required within professions. Yet, by virtue of their position within the community, professionals have responsibilities to help maintain the vitality and integrity of its public affairs. The license to practice has always entailed the concept of social obligation. Democracy must mean more to a professional than merely the form of government allowing one to seek the good life in his own way (Smith, 1939, p. 6). Similarly, in Adult Basic Education or Adult Vocational Education learners should be provided with intellectual skills necessary to fulfill their functions as citizens. Democracy is the necessary context that makes their ambitions as professionals or union members or parents attainable. Civic competence and civic virtue should not be preempted by other educational purposes, no matter how worthy or lucrative. In a democracy, the office of citizen is supreme.

Adult civic education means the purposeful and systematic effort to develop in adults the skills and dispositions to function effectively as citizens in their communities as well as in the larger world. The purpose is to both develop understanding and judgment about public issues and to contribute to guided and informed decisions and actions through deliberation, public talk, and dialogue. Deciding and acting are forms of participation. Increasing participation in the democratic process and using such participation as a catalyst for learning are desirable outcomes of adult civic education. To decide and to act is also to choose and choosing wisely involves making inchoate values explicit. In the past new agencies have been created or existing Adult Education agencies have adapted themselves to accomplish this purpose. What has been learned from those initiatives and the theoretical foundation on which they were based will serve to inform this treatise.

Several authors have delineated the goals of civic education for children. For example, Richard Pratte says that the goal is, "The development of citizens who choose to act reasonably, intelligently, and creatively while manifesting a sense of fairness, obligation, or duty to others" (1988, p. 162). R. Freeman Butts says the goal is, "To motivate students and enable them to play their parts as informed, responsible, committed, and effective members of a modern democratic political system" (1980, p. 132). And Richard Remy says succinctly that, "Citizenship education involves learning and instruction related to the development of citizen competence" (1980, p. 1). More recently, the social organization of schools and the classroom has come to be recognized as part of the citizenship curriculum.

In order for school-based civic education to bear fruit, maturity and learning must continue throughout life. Adult Education agencies can continue the process in several ways. First, such agencies can provide consultative and support services to augment the learning resulting from efforts of citizens already participating in public dialogue. For example, an Adult Education agency may be able to assist rural property owners living near an expanding urban community who are attempting to understand the criteria used by local government to determine whether to grant variances in the zoning code requested by land developers. Second, Adult Education agencies can integrate civic content and issues into existing programs. Third, forums and seminars on specific topics of concern to citizens, such as solid waste disposal and catastrophic health insurance can be added to the curriculum. At all times the goal should be to nourish in ordinary citizens the knowledge and skills required for intelligent public deliberation and choice in matters related to the common good.

OBSTACLES TO ADULT CIVIC EDUCATION

This important educational task of helping adults acquire the competence necessary to play an active part in public affairs and also accept the obligation to do so has formidable obstacles. First, there are attitudinal problems. Pursuit of self-interest and individual advantage at the expense of weaker persons or groups is more characteristic of contemporary citizen behavior. In *CommonWealth,* Harry Boyte (1989) says that adults live in a "Litigious society of confrontations and special interests that results in civic suffocation" (p. 6). Even citizen action, focusing as it often does on specific and narrow issues, has neglected to connect its goals to any broader social or political vision, and has failed to relate newly acquired political skills to larger community problems. Then, there is the reluctance on the part of Adult Education agencies to make community improvement or social change or social action anything more than pleasant sounding phrases to round out publicity brochures. In addition, because society is increasingly complex, there is the tendency on the part of citizens and elected officials alike to defer to the "tyranny of experts."

Regrettably, Adult Education agencies have avoided engagement with the turbulant political world of choices and dilemmas associated with citizenship, preferring instead the placid environment of academic subject matter, certificates, and diplomas. Except in public relations bulletins and mission statements, the lexicon of adult education no longer contains terms such as community development, social action, social change, and civic improvement. These rich categories have been surplanted by terms such as organizational efficiency, employee productivity, workplace literacy, and personal enrichment. By neglecting education regarding the gritty problems and ethical issues faced by citizens and governments, Adult Education agencies have relegated themselves to the sidelines and become peripheral observers to the task of establishing a democratic civic culture.

THE CENTRAL THESIS

The central thesis of *Adult Civic Education* is that instead of being deaf to the argument, debate, dialogue, and conflict that surrounds the political questions of civic life, Adult Education agencies should facilitate understanding of community problems and choices, equip citizens to participate intelligently and skillfully in the democratic process, and augment the learning that accrues from such participation with opportunities to reflect and dialogue about the experience. Barber (1984) emphasizes the opportunities for civic education that are embedded in participation in democracy. "Strong democracy relies on participation in an evolving problem-solving community that creates public ends where there were none before by means of its own activity.... Community grows out of participation and at the same time makes participation possible; civic activity educates individuals how to think publicly as citizens" (p. 152).

Two correlates follow closely upon this civic educational imperative. First, specific dimensions of citizenship that compel adults to continue learning will be suggested. Second, possible activities and interventions to enhance civic virtue and competence that Adult Education agencies can provide will be identified and described. Boyte (1988) explores the responsibilities and capabilities of citizens as agents of democracy in an "information age." His thesis is that effective citizenship is possible if, and only if, "Citizens develop the abilities to gain access to information of all kinds ... and the skills to put such information to effective use. Moreover, the possibilities for a reinvigorated popular sovereignty are dependent not only on information and knowledge but also on what might best be called 'wisdom': the ability to *guide* and frame action with integrative concepts and a clear, if flexible and evolving, set of public values and purposes" (p. 5). Thus knowledge about often increasingly technical issues, as a resource to be shared by citizens as well as values, virtue, and moral judgements of political actions, are all inescapable elements in citizenship. They are also all part of what goes into civic education.

Allowing for the sex, race, and social status biases that were prevalent in his time, Thomas Jefferson was America's earliest proponent of the symbiotic relationship between education and citizenship. In a letter to William C. Jarvis, dated September 28, 1820, Jefferson wrote of the close bond that must exist between representative government and popular enlightenment, between a viable democracy and intelligent popular rule. "I know of no safe depository of the ultimate powers of the society but the people themselves; and if we think them not enlightened enough to exercise their control with a wholesome discretion, the remedy is not to take it from them, but to inform their discretion by education" (Lee, 1961, p. 17). Education for Jefferson and the other founding fathers involved knowledge of the insights available from a thorough grounding in the humanities disciplines of philosophy, history, and literature.

THE EFFICACY OF SCHOOL-BASED CIVIC EDUCATION

The urgency of civic education in the adult years is made all the more paramount when the efficacy of the school-based effort is examined. In survey after survey, American high school and college students find the civics portions of standardized tests to be the most difficult. Boyte writes, "Not only did Americans participate less in the political system (in the 1988 presidential election), many also lacked the basic information necessary to judge and analyze events, issues, and rhetoric. 'Citizenship' was boring and 'politics' had become . . . a disparaging epithet. Studies suggested a widespread lack of knowledge about history, geography, and political structures. Americans endorsed democratic norms in the abstract, but support for elemental liberties dropped precipitously when people were asked to consider specific, emotion-laden cases or even the Bill of Rights" (1989, p. 2). Morris Janowitz (1983) reports that he and colleagues surveyed undergraduates in 1979 concerning their attitudes towards nine rights and nine obligations. The four key citizen rights (freedom of speech, choice of religion, right to vote, and right to a trial by jury) were accorded the greatest importance, higher than that given to any obligation. Not only was no civic obligation rated as important as any one of the four traditional political rights, but several obligations were rated as much less important than all other rights. The duty to educate one's children to civic responsibility, the duty to vote, and the duty to pay taxes were the three highest rated obligations. It is significant to note says Janowitz, that the right to vote is rated higher than the duty to vote; and the right to a speedy trial by jury is considered more important than the obligation to serve on a jury.

Ten years later, Broder reported that a recent survey of college students conducted by pollster Peter Hart ("Democracy's next generation"), indicated greater knowledge and appreciation of rights than requirements of citizenship. Broder says that, "The concept of 'good citizenship' these young people have gained is individualistic—not civic. Asked how they would describe a 'good citizen' in their own words, the dominant answer (43%) was that it meant someone who is generous and caring. Only one-third mentioned being law-abiding and only 12 percent suggested voting or other forms of political involvement" (Washington Post, 11/29/89, p. 27A). The emphasis on self-fulfillment, so natural to youth, is crowding out a sense of involvement with the community and nation. Broder concludes by observing that "one way or another we have to find a way to teach this generation the other half of democracy's story: the experience of civic involvement and citizenship obligation."

The National Center for Education Statistics (1978) concluded its 1969 to 1976 study of changes in political knowledge and attitudes of 17 year olds with several distressing general comments. The report concludes: "The decline in knowledge about the structure and function of government and the essential concepts underlying democracy is most disappointing and should be cause for a hard reassessment of the social studies curriculum" (p. 59). Even more pertinent to our purposes its authors go on to speculate that, "Students' declining political participation may reflect the attitudes of the adult society. The 1970s have seen an increasing preoccupation with personal goals, a general disillusionment with the political process and a trend toward conservatism. It is not surprising that youths have been influenced by these tendencies. . . . Education for citizenship does not take place only in the schools. Young people learn values and attitudes related to citizenship from their families, their peers, their communities and the media. If the values of the society and the values taught by the schools are in conflict, the schools cannot be expected to counteract single-handedly the values and attitudes conveyed by the society at large. . . . Preparing youth for citizenship is terribly basic, but community pressure is generally focused on improving the quality of education in mathematics and reading and often ignores attention to citizenship education" (pp. 60–61).

The most recent study to confirm this dismal portrait of declining interest in civic matters was released June 28, 1990 by the Times Mirror Center for the People and the Press. Its authors, Donald D. Kellermann, Andrew Kohut, and Carol Bowerman found young adults, from 18 to 29 years of age, to be a generation that "knows less, cares less, votes less, and is less critical of its leaders and institutions than young people in the past." It is difficult to estimate the contribution that curriculum in Adult

Education agencies has made to this preoccupation with personal goals at the expense of education in responsibility for the common good.

ADULTS ARE RESPONSIBLE FOR DEMOCRACY

Ultimately it is adults who must practice democracy. It is adults who require information about complex local and national issues from air quality to zoning, and who require skills and wisdom to put the information to effective use. As voters and decision makers adults determine the quality of democratic society. What was learned in school, in this sphere as in every other dimension of modern life, is insufficient to sustain a person for a life-time of participation in democracy. Through decisions and attitudes adults reflect notions of the commonwealth, perhaps hazily or sharply defined, and what is in its best interests. A democratic society is fashioned to reflect the vision, will, and purposes of its members. It is obvious, however, that many are not swayed by the concept of public responsibility for the common good.

It is sometimes erroneously assumed that the solution to civic disinterest is to increase voter turnout. If only a larger percentage of those eligible to vote could be shamed, scolded, or cajoled to do so then the defects of democracy would be removed. So periodically state legislatures and the Congress enact measures to make it easier to register to vote. Experience shows, however, that such measures do not appreciably increase voter participation.

In reality the slacker vote is not a disease but a symptom. The disease is more obscure and intransigent. It has to do first, with superficial understanding by citizens that government is the tool or instrument to carry out their will. Second, it represents a failure of will to take collective responsibility for things pertaining to the common good. Third, it indicates inability or unwillingness to examine and confront the values embedded in conflicts and problems as well as the choices to be made to resolve them. Furthermore, it has never been assumed that voter participation in and of itself will ensure that democracy works. Rather, it is informed participation, informed choices made after study and deliberation that is the foundation for democracy. Not surprisingly, persons concerned with the endurance of democracy despair of ever appreciably improving citizen behavior. Instead of concentrating on improving citizen judgement and discretion, they focus on the preparation of better leaders. This is the position taken by a major school of democratic theory to be examined in the next chapter.

Civic education promotes engagement in community objectives and problems as virtuous. But as Pratte (1988) indicates, "The rub is that many are committed to individualism and to an individualistic logic, asserted in terms of autonomy, self-reliance, getting ahead, and keeping ahead of others, regardless of the cost in human suffering; and they therefore deny the value of the public good" (p. 16). It is expressed in sentiments such as, Why should I vote for school levies when I have no children in school? Why should I support public transit when I don't use it. Civic education, on the other hand, strives to develop what Barber (1984) calls "we-thinkers." "The citizen is by definition a *we*-thinker, and to think of the *we* is always to transform how interests are perceived and goods defined. . . . participation is a way of defining the self, just as citizenship is a way of living" (p. 153).

A CONCEPTUAL BASE FOR ADULT CIVIC EDUCATION

As a field of study and practice, adult education is conceptually eclectic. Diverse theories of learning, human development, and business management undergird most of the research and practice on learning, instruction, and administration. Similarly, the theoretical framework for determining the scope of adult civic education is derived from scholarship on democracy and citizenship that provides the rationale for civic rights and responsibilities. Perhaps the rich tradition in the United States, dating at least from the 1920s, of Adult Education agencies facilitating social change, social reform, and political action is rapidly vanishing because of a lack of consensus among scholars as well as the general public over the meaning of democracy and the roles of citizens within it.

It is generally believed that the pursuit of social and political purposes described in adult education literature both involved the practice of effective citizenship and resulted in further civic learning for the participants. Certainly adults must both draw upon and augment their school-based knowledge of civics in order to participate effectively in the democratic process. Participation itself involves learning by doing. Reading and interpreting large amounts of technical information, reconciling the conflicting values embedded in questions and choices, and dealing with controversy and uncertainty are often factors influencing the learning process. An objective of this book is to contribute to an understanding of the vehicles available to autonomous citizens who desire to continue their civic education beyond formal schooling, and specifically, the contribution that adult education agencies can make to this process. That scholarship has been largely unformed, or perhaps dormant.

An additional objective is to explore the rich context for understanding public problems and choices afforded by the humanities. The thesis advanced here is that the humanities offer help with conducting the business of democracy. They present an array of perspectives for discussion and dialogue about public issues and choices without imposing solutions. The humanities are the tools of citizenship that enable citizens to enlighten opinion and passion with reflection and reason.

Obtaining and applying the knowledge necessary to successfully fulfill the rights and obligations of citizenship should not be left to chance. An explicit assumption on which this book is based is: *Adult Education agencies can and should intervene to accomplish fundamental attitudinal change of free men and women regarding their role as citizen, the highest political office in the land.* Adult education agencies are uniquely positioned to provide the knowledge and skills, and to promote the civic-minded attitudes necessary for the tasks of choosing and working towards community priorities. Such agencies can have no higher purpose than to promote the attitudes and skills necessary for participation and involvement in a democratic society and to augment the learning that accrues when these behaviors occur.

In adult education ideology, and often in practice, participation through discussion and dialogue are at the heart of the process and the lexicon. In a monograph written for the Ohio Humanities Council, Charles Cole (1988) advocates such learning methods for its educational programs. "Programs which generate meaningful audience discussion are likely to be most successful in producing active group learning. They are also likely to be the most successful in meeting the goals of the state humanities councils and in producing greatest audience satisfaction" (p. 8). There is a marvelous confluence and symmetry of methods and purposes in democracy and adult education, especially when the humanities are the wellspring for learning. Participation through discussion as a prelude to action is at the heart of both adult education and democracy. However, in neither case can such behaviors go unexercised. As with any skills, those pertinent to democratic citizenship cannot be presumed if left dormant. They must be maintained through use and sharpened through intellectual discourse, a task to which Adult Education agencies should dedicate themselves.

REFERENCES

Barber, Benjamin R. (1984). *Strong Democracy.* Berkeley, University of California Press.

Boyte, Harry C. (1989). *CommonWealth.* New York, The Free Press.

Broder, David. (November 29, 1989). Washington Post, p. 27A.

Butts, R. Freeman. (1988). *The Morality of Democratic Citizenship.* Calabasas, CA, Center for Civic Education.

Cole, Charles C. Jr. (1988). *A Handbook on Adult Learning.* Columbus, Ohio Humanities Council.

Janowitz, Morris. (1983). *The Reconstruction of Patriotism.* Chicago, University of Chicago Press.

Kellermann, Donald S., Kohut, Andrew, and Bowman, Carol. (1990). *The Age of Indifference.* Washington, D.C., Times Mirror Center for the People and the Press.

Lee, G.C. (Editor). (1961). *Crusade Against Ignorance: Thomas Jefferson on Education.* Classics in Education, No. 6, New York, Teachers College Press.

National Center for Education Statistics. (1978). *Changes in Political Knowledge and Attitudes, 1969-1976.* Citizenship/Social Studies Report 07-CS-02, Denver, Educational Commission of the States.

Pratte, Richard. (1988). *The Civic Imperative.* New York, Teachers College Press, Columbia University.

Remy, Richard C. (1980). *Handbook of Basic Citizenship Competencies.* Alexandria, Association for Supervision and Curriculum Development.

Smith, Thomas V. (1939). *The Democratic Way of Life.* Chicago, University of Chicago Press.

Chapter 2

THE MEANING OF DEMOCRACY
AND CITIZENSHIP

When they arrested me
(the last time) on October 27, 1989) . . .
our society slumbered beneath the pall of a
totalitarian system. Today . . . I am speaking to
you as the representative of a country that has set
out on the road to democracy, a country where there is
complete freedom of speech, which is getting ready for free
elections, and . . . wants to create a prosperous market economy.

Vaclav Havel, President
Czechoslovak Socialist Republic
Address to United States Congress
February 21, 1990

The yearning for freedom is timeless, universal, and unquenchable.
Witness the events in the Spring 1989. For two short weeks courageous Chinese students in Tiananmen Square, Beijing captured the
attention and admiration of the Western world. They literally starved
themselves for piecemeal democracy. Their crude replicas of the goddess
of Liberty were redolent symbols of freedoms craved. It seems reasonable to wonder, however, what democracy could mean to persons without
experience or practice in it? Besides the desire for freedom to assemble
and speak openly, what else did those students and their countrymen
understand democracy to mean? How accurate or fanciful could their
notions be of what is required to sustain it? Furthermore, if we who are
practiced in democracy were able to give them a crash course in its inner
workings and what is expected of its citizens, where would we start?

The questions posed above about the students in China are salient for
the residents of central and eastern Europe as well where the grip of
totalitarian governments in the Warsaw Pact has been broken and the
Iron Curtain has come unraveled. Citizens of countries with precious
little experience or tradition of self-rule are assembling to demand the

reforms that lead to freely elected governments. As David Broder explains, "None (of these countries) has a wide variety of pluralistic institutions to give voice to people's concerns; none has professional and competitive news organizations, independent of government or party control, committed to informing the citizenry; none has legislators and government officials with the know-how and equipment to make a truly representative government work" (Washington Post, 12/31/89, p. 7C). When people grow up under a system in which the government is the agent for choosing and directing all facets of life, how do ordinary citizens suddenly learn to be autonomous, to be citizens, to govern, to choose, to establish community priorities, and to direct government as the instrument of their purposes? The temptation to succumb to native fascism will be strong. As Janowitz (1983) maintains, there is a long, tortured process of societal transformation by which "subjects" become "citizens." That transition will occupy eastern European nations for years to come.

The present Herculean struggle to fashion democratically constituted governments in erstwhile totalitarian states prompts reflection upon the public's role as citizens in all countries. It is an occasion to examine the knowledge, skills, attitudes, and forms of participation required of citizens in order to sustain a free society and the methods for attaining them. Again, as with the Chinese students, it can be asked, what might Americans say to central and eastern Europeans about the behaviors and knowledge necessary to sustain a free, open, and participatory society? Citizenship is a dynamic concept, fecund with a variety of meanings, a subject of continuous debate, and undergoing extensive modifications from its Graeco-Roman origins, to the founders of the United States, to the twenty-first century when it will again need to be reformulated to take account of contemporary political, economic, and social conditions. Historically, adults in the United States have both drawn upon and augmented their school-based knowledge of civics by participating in their communities and in the democratic process in a variety of ways. Volunteering, recycling waste, serving on community boards, providing leadership to youth groups, voting, supporting political candidates, running for office, attending and contributing to hearings or committee meetings of official government bodies, serving as citizen representatives on government committees, and contributing time and talent to citizen action groups attempting to influence business, industry, or government policy are forms of civic participation.

Learning has always been central to effective participation. Extensive technical information and many contending groups with conflicting values and articulate spokespersons are often ingredients in the process. In participating, citizens attempt to achieve rough epistemological parity with professionals, public relations experts, government bureaucrats, elected officials, and technicians. Participation in these activities has been the "university" for studying and learning both the community and democracy. In addition, Adult Education agencies, have to some extent facilitated the learning that accrues through participation in the community and the democratic process through purposeful and systematic educational programs and services. In fact, there is a long tradition in adult education literature and practice of using education as a means to facilitate social change, social reform, political action, and civic improvement. While the mix of education and action has varied, improving the abilities of citizens to act collectively in an enlightened manner, and to create organizational structures for furthering their purposes have been acceptable educational goals. The pursuit of social and political purposes both involved the practice of effective citizenship and resulted in further civic learning for the participants.

Ironically, as people in other countries hasten to embrace democracy there is cause to wonder and doubt whether Americans are in a position to teach them anything about it. Democratic theorists such as Boyte (1989) suggest that the American body politic is in disarray because of a profound disengagement from community affairs, from politics, and from public life. Volunteering is a casualty of busy life styles. Voting, the minimum form of participation in a democracy, was at its lowest level in the November 1988 elections since 1924. Furthermore, in recent presidential elections, thoughtful reflection and reasoned dialogue among voters have been casualties of the substitution of symbols for substance and 30-second television sound bites for authentic debate. Nor do elected officials speak with eloquence or ferocity about individual citizen responsibility. Contrast the blame-shifting timidity of our national leaders with the personal courage of Poland's Lech Walesa or South Africa's Nelson Mandella or Czechoslovakia's President Vaclav Havel who, in Havel's words, have been "pinned under a boulder" and have felt the machinery of the police state rumble over them. In his address to the Congress, without the slightest trace of self-righteousness, Havel gently chastised us all for "reprehensible passivity" in the face of totalitarian governments.

Concurrent with this widespread disaffection with civic concerns and decline in civic literacy, efforts by Adult Education agencies to assist persons with learning necessary to engage more effectively in the democratic process and in community action or community development projects have, not surprisingly, all but disappeared. In place of civic education less controversial and more lucrative purposes such as corporate efficiency, economic development, professional improvement, and personal enrichment have assumed prominence in the curriculum of educational programs for adults. Nor does the curriculum available from Adult Education agencies attempt to integrate civic concerns as a part of professional competence, corporate behavior, or personal development.

Then there is the issue of the professional Adult Education literature. Not surprisingly, it has become almost exclusively concerned with the technical arcana of managing the enterprise or generic questions of learning theory, motivation, participation, and the like. Normative considerations regarding the obligations of Adult Education agencies to the larger society are rare. Meanwhile, many lament what Jack Mezirow (1989), Professor of Adult Education at Columbia Teachers College in a letter to professor colleagues called, " . . . the drift of the field of Adult Education from its original concern as an enterprise driven by social ideals to one overwhelmingly market driven." In effect, by avoiding civic education, agencies concerned with the learning needs of adults relegate themselves to the sidelines and become peripheral observers in this important sphere of life. Indeed, adult civic education has been diminished as a means to counter citizen apathy, selfishness, and powerlessness and as an antidote to autocratic, special-interest, or elitist authority. Whereas the need to revive the promise that adult education holds for strengthening democracy, promoting social action, encouraging critical discourse on public issues, and promoting civic virtue remains strong.

THE POLITICAL CONDITION

It is impossible to value and promote democracy and community involvement without also being concerned with citizenship and politics. They are inextricably intertwined. In a democracy citizens share custody of the commonwealth and citizenship refers to the capacity to influence politics. The realm of politics involves action, choice, and conflict. Politics does not necessarily mean government. Just living together and belonging to groups makes politics necessary. As Robert Woyach (1989) explains, "It is through politics that groups or communities determine the criteria for distributing values among members. Politics allows free people living in groups to create shared goals, to come to common understandings of needs, and to pool their resources to accomplish shared images of the future. Politics is not a process reserved to government; it is part of everyday life. Without politics a group cannot make decisions. Unless it accepts authoritarian rule, it cannot act as a group. Groups and communities that cannot decide or act ultimately die" (p. 14). David Matthews (1989) says that through politics we decide who we are and what kind of society is best. According to Easton (1966, p. 2) the essence of politics is social interactions on the part of individuals and groups for the purpose of authoritatively allocating valued things for a society.

Yet, contrast this appreciation for the political process as a necessary and important part of adult behavior with the evidence, documented by both William Griffith (1976) and David Stewart (1982) that adult educators abhor it as something beneath them—dirty, unseemly, to be avoided at all costs. Is it any wonder that agencies concerned with the learning needs of adults have forfeited responsibility for helping their clients with the task of defining the common good and setting the public agenda?

In an extensive treatise on the many forms democracy assumes, Barber (1984) describes what he calls the "political condition." It is a condition that must be fully appreciated by those who would promote adult civic education. First, politics is action undertaken by a public and intended to have public consequences. Thus only a citizen can be a political actor. Second, to be political is to choose with deliberation and responsibility. Action that is impulsive, arbitrary, or unconsidered is not political action. To speak, says Barber, of those who choose with deliberation and act with responsibility is, in the political realm, to speak of citizens. Third, and of particular consequence for civic education, the deciding that citizens and elected officials must do has to proceed without certitude or assurance that one course of action is inherently better than another. That is, there is no independent ground, no external standard standard to apply to attain certitude. Neither science, nor philosophy, nor religion can answer whether to raise taxes, form a neighborhood crime watch, start a civic association, oppose a rezoning initiative, establish a bird sanctuary, fire the police chief, extend the sewer system, wage war, annex land, build a hospital or any other of the myriad questions facing citizens and elected officials. Final Truth remains forever beyond the reach of politics. Finally, a source of special nervousness to educators is that these choices are almost always made in the presence of conflict. They involve power, special interests, and value differences.

The choice Barber says, comes in the form of, "What shall we do when something has to be done that affects us all, we wish to be reasonable, yet we disagree on means and ends and are without independent grounds for making the choice?" (1984, p. 120). This is choosing under the worst possible circumstances, without guiding standards and when doing nothing itself carries consequences. When there is certain knowledge there is no conflict, and therefore no need of politics. When consensus stops, politics begins. It bears repeating that all the important choices facing communities require politics and the skills and knowledge that go into defining the common good. Only some of these choices involve government.

Barber reviews the democratic responses that have evolved to cope with the "political condition" and asserts that not all of them are equally receptive to full participation by citizens. He then advocates "strong democracy" as an ideal in which civic education throughout the lifespan, citizen participation, and public deliberation are essential ingredients. Each of these elements is intertwined with the others and mutually interdependent. For citizens, "Participation has as its primary function the education of judgement. The citizen is the individual who has learned how to make civic judgements and who can evaluate goods in public terms" (p. 158).

The task then for democracy and adult civic education is to find ways to nurture judgement and action in the face of uncertainty. In strong democracy, knowledge is essential and it is knowledge of which adults alone are capable. Unlike the knowledge that can be obtained from books or the minds of experts, civic and, of course, political knowledge is epistemologically autonomous. That is, it has no tests of certitude other than those created by consensus and application. This kind of thinking, judging, and deciding is experiential. There are no "true" or "false" answers or positions, only alternative visions that compete for acceptance. This kind of knowledge, democratic knowledge, is also provisional, in that it adapts to evolving priorities and communal purposes. "Creativity and the capacity to see anew, to see empathetically, become the special virtues of an effective political epistemology. For the challenge is to envision the human future and then to inspire a passion in others for that vision (p. 170).

Whether in politics, education, or any of the organizations and institutions that make up the civic community, participation implies direct engagement of the deliberating mind and the choosing will. While the masses may lack purpose and direction, participants in democracy and in educational enterprises cannot. As with learning, politics is something done by, not to, citizens. Involvement, commitment, common deliberation, and common work characterize the participants in both. Service and obligation are often motives behind both. In strong democracy lifelong civic education is both an outcome and a prerequisite of enlightened civic participation.

The events in central and eastern Europe in 1989 and continuing in this decade are instructive. They serve as reminders that only citizens can supply consensus for the kind of society in which they prefer to live. And even democratic governments cannot define their own purposes. They require the people to chart their course and to define the standards for them to follow. In a democracy it is citizens who carry the burden of governance, seeking the necessary knowledge to make enlightened choices among competing purposes. Government is the instrument used by citizens to achieve their goals. Furthermore, democratic communities, according to Matthews (1989), require a civic infrastructure—a host of nongovernmental associations—that take on some of the responsibility for the management of society as a whole. These educational, political, religious, and civic associations, in Matthew's words, "Provide public environments in which people are able to learn a new self-respect, a deeper and more assertive group identity, public skills, the values of cooperation, and civic virtues" (p. 82). The nearly wholesale abandonment of civic education by agencies purporting to serve the learning needs of adults leaves an immense void in the civic infrastructure.

CITIZENSHIP AS A BALANCE
OF RIGHTS AND OBLIGATIONS

An excessively individualist bias in American society makes it increasingly important to democracy to determine what and who is the public and what are public roles. A casualty of this bias is that the concept of "citizen" is detached from any communal ties or civic obligations. There are widespread tendencies first, to privatize things that have heretofore been public, second, to place a higher premium on private rights than public and social obligations, third, to not see connections between private interests and public policy issues, and fourth, to allow special interests to suprecede the public good. Citizenship is increasingly understood as a corpus of rights, such as to vote, assemble, and speak freely. Citizenship theorists on the other hand contend it involves a balance between rights and obligations. Janowitz (1983) draws the distinction. "By rights I mean the legal, political, and socioeconomic prerogatives that the person enjoys because of the collective action of the political system. By civic obligations I mean the contributions and sacrifices a citizen makes to keep the political system effective. Those obligations are designed to prevent or thwart autocratic rule" (p. 2).

The current, almost grotesque emphasis on the rights of citizenship versus obligations is a natural expression of the belief system which characterized the 1980s. Greed, selfishness, and ostentation embodied much of the ethic of the "Me Decade." Dramatic examples of corruption in the nation's political and business dealings convey a diminished concept of responsibility for the common good. An excessively individualist bias that gradually detaches citizens from concern for the common good or communal obligations has held sway for some time now. Bellah and Associates (1985) concluded their examination of American culture with the lament that a "cancerous individualism" was destroying the country's older language of civic commitment. Boyte (1989) complains that the historical notion of commonwealth as a self-governing community of equals concerned about the general welfare and assuming responsibility over its basic resources and public goods has largely disappeared from our public vocabulary over the past generation. Woyach (1989) says that the chief failing of our political system has been, " . . . its inability to encourage average citizens to participate in the search for the public good" (p. 16).

Patriotism by and large does not extend to defining the public good in terms other than what coincides with private interests. It is left to elected officials to articulate a vision of the public good. Most citizens lack the skills necessary to participate in defining it, and the question candidates for public office hear most often is, "What will you do for me if you get elected?" No wonder the "vision thing" has not fared well in recent years. The ascendancy of special as well as private interests in the political realm contributes to civic suffocation.

Excessive individualism has given rise to what Barber (1984, p. 142) labels as *juridical democracy,* defined by the arbitration, adjudication, and protection of rights by a representative but independent judiciary that governs indirectly by placing limits on the government. The law and the Constitution are invoked as independent grounds for settling conflict. Citizens desist from public activity and the civic learning it requires in deference to the judicial process. And both legislators and citizens increasingly defer to the courts as a policy-making body.

In Barber's conceptual frame another response to the "political condition" is what he calls *pluralist democracy.* American economic practice extols private enterprise in which individuals separately and collectively compete for success in the marketplace. This commercial pluralism is mirrored in free market politics where special interests compete for advantage in the legislative process through competitive lobbying and bargaining. Citizens are active but fragmented.

The chief deficiency of pluralist democracy, according to Barber, is the absence, indeed often the inability of citizens to generate public thinking or public ends of any kind. Citizen talent, energy, and intelligence are siphoned off and exclusively devoted to pursuit of private interests. Somehow it is fallaciously assumed that, in addition to private interests, or perhaps as a by-product of them, the public good will also be served. In the main, it is not public purposes but rather those of large, organized, wealthy, vocal, and private constituencies that are served best. It is no wonder then that in the United States people equate the political process with unethical deal making. Disassociation with anything political is raised to the level of virtue. Educators in particular are prone to position themselves "above" this murky arena where basic values risk being compromised.

WHAT AND WHO IS THE PUBLIC?

Since the public is essential to democracy, it is necessary to determine what and who is the public and what are public roles. The nature of publicness is explained by David Matthews (1987) in *The Promise of Democracy,* a source book for use with the National Issues Forums. Matthews carefully distinguishes the concept of public from what is ordinary or open to everyone, from a mass or crowd, and from government itself. Instead he equates public with a group of people having a certain connection to one another, a relationship of interdependence among strangers sharing common objectives. "Our public life is our shared life in all its forms" (p. 30). It is political in the broadest sense. The public realm is more basic than the realm of government because it sets direction and steers a course for government. Government is its instrument. "To be fully public is to be cognizant of the reality of our interdependence. It is to be as aware as we can be of the consequences of our actions on the whole of the political community" (p. 40). In fact, the vitality and health of the much glorified private sector is dependent on the public sphere. According to Matthews, the public realm is the environment in which the private exists. It is the water we drink, which if polluted, causes everyone to suffer.

Matthews emphasizes the public or pregovernmental origins of democracy, beginning the story, not in 1776 or 1787, but in 1633 with town meetings called to resolve common or public problems. In these meetings, people defined their common, shared purposes and a tradition of public talk in public places was developed. The faith in the Revolution expressed by both Samuel Adams and Thomas Jefferson can be attributed to what each learned about people and the power of their public halls.

After the War for Independence, Matthews goes on to point out, these same town meetings were the forum for the people to take charge of their future. Through public talk they debated, modified, and finally accepted their separate state constitutions, and ultimately, the U.S. Constitution. Hannah Arendt (1963) observes that unlike the constitutions emerging from other nations then, or now, "Ours was the product of rough-and-tumble serious public scrutiny, created by talk, and, with the addition of the Bill of Rights, explicitly protecting talk—in the right to assemble and to speak freely" (p. 25).

CONFLICTING THEORIES OF DEMOCRACY AND CITIZENSHIP

It is a premise of *Adult Civic Education* that disengagement by citizens from politics and public issues—phenomena inimical to early democratic practices in this country, are indicative of a not so subtle shift in the meaning of democracy. This shift is conveyed in the different views about significance of citizen participation in Contemporary versus Classical democratic theory. Such theoretical differences are important because inevitably education reflects philosophical creed and serves to promote or emphasize one version or another of a democratic society and what is required of citizens to maintain it. In Classical democracy the idea of maximum participation of all the people in governance is central. This theoretical position has been severely criticized, first, because of its normative dimension, and second, because it is said to be hopelessly unrealistic. Initiated by Schumpeter (1943) and endorsed by numerous others, the criticism asserts that democratic theory should be scientific and empirical, value-free and descriptive. Democracy is not an ideal end or an end at all. Rather, it is a means, a method for arriving at political decisions. Its most vital feature is competition by potential decision makers for the people's vote.

According to Pateman (1970), Schumpeter compared political competition for votes to the operation of an economic market; voters, like consumers, choose between the policies (products) offered by competing political entrepreneurs and the parties regulate the competition. This interpretation of democracy has gradually come to enjoy near universal acceptance by theorists. Evidence of this can be found in contemporary political science with its emphasis on empirical studies of voting trends and the absence of political philosophy, by practices of modern-day political operatives and media specialists to market candidates based on feedback from polls and focus groups.

Contemporary Democratic Theory

Pateman examines the work of three well known scholars (Berelson, 1954; Dahl, 1956; Sartori, 1962) to document the increasing acceptance of the Schumpeter or Contemporary school of thought. Each of these three democratic theorists depreciates the significance of citizen participation in governance in favor of the centrality of elected leadership. Impressed by the need for leadership and disillusioned by the failure of many citizens to engage actively and responsibly in politics, these theorists have shifted their foci from the ordinary citizen to their elected representatives. The "electoral mass" is incapable of action other than a stampede. It is leaders who must be active, initiate, decide. Thus limited participation and voter apathy have a positive contribution. They cushion the functions of government from the shock of widespread interference, disagreement, adjustment, and change. High levels of participation and interest are required from only a minority of citizens. Control of the leaders and the system is exercised in the electoral competition among leaders for the votes of those who do participate and the sanction of removal from office.

Fortunately, according to Contemporary democratic theorists, the average citizen only reacts to the initiatives and policies of competing elites and their leaders. Besides, the incredible complexity of most issues facing government at all levels today defies comprehension by the average citizen. The judgements of technical specialists, not those of average citizens, are indispensable to the deliberations of elected officials and government administrators. In fact, it is the view of these theorists that citizens just get in the way and complicate the decision-making process. Naturally, Contemporary theory stresses the importance of improving the quality of leaders and the conditions under which they operate. Whereas the weaknesses of citizens, particularly their lack of information and understanding, are skirted, not ameliorated. No significant institution in society has emerged to correct this imbalance. To attempt to reduce apathy and ignorance through such means as adult civic education, for example, would endanger the stability of the democratic method. Contemporary democratic theory embraces the trend toward centralized, bureaucratic power that emasculates citizens and discourages their involvement in government. The participation of citizens is limited to choosing leaders, thus protecting themselves from arbitrary and corrupt elected officials.

Pateman's thesis is that Schumpeter and his followers, though influential, have misunderstood and distorted the meaning of Classical democracy and the role of citizens. Schumpeter defined Classical democracy as, "That institutional arrangement for arriving at political decisions which realizes the common good by making the people itself decide issues through the election of individuals who are to assemble in order to carry out its will" (1943, p. 250). Maximum participation of all the people is central to it, as is rational, active, and informed participation. This is asking too much of the ordinary citizen, say the Contemporary theorists. To illustrate, Pateman quotes Sartori: "On the whole, when the ordinary man has to deal with political affairs the sense of reality is completely lost and he drops to a lower level of mental performance as soon as he enters the political field." Thus Sartori accounts for the voter who judges candidates according to which one rang my doorbell last and who judges issues by whatever my barber thinks.

Classical Democratic Theory

Pateman reviews the work of three earlier theorists—Rousseau (1968), J.S. Mill (1963), and G.D.H. Cole (1913; 1920)—in order to develop a fuller and richer interpretation of Classical democracy and refute what she contends are the distortions of the Contemporary school. It is the position of Classical democracy that far wider participatory functions are called for than merely choosing leaders in free elections. Participation is central to the establishment and maintenance of a democratic polity. For Rousseau, participation means being involved in making decisions and thereby ensuring good government. But more than this and central to the focus of *Adult Civic Education,* is the educative function of participation. Educative in the widest sense because through participation citizens find that they must take into account wider matters than their own immediate, private interests if the support of others is to be obtained. The result is the emergence of civic virtue and the necessity to nurture it.

Pateman paraphrases Rousseau to say that as a result of participating in decision making through various forms of citizen action, as opposed to entrusting the process to elected leaders and the technical experts on whom they rely, citizens learn to distinguish between personal desires and the common good. Furthermore, the participatory process is self-sustaining and reinforcing, in that competence is enhanced through practice and citizens gain real influence and sometimes even control over the network of governmental structures influencing their lives. In contrast, it is the failure of those institutions and structures to encourage or permit citizen participation that poses the greatest threat to freedom. The major educative functions of participation occur in three ways. First, citizens learn that being their own masters requires digging for information and knowing what they are talking about. Second, through the participatory process citizens learn that no person or group is in a position to know everything and be master of another. Third, citizens learn that they "belong" in their community and it belongs to them. Fourth, they learn that by being knowledgeable, persistent, and willing to take a variety of overt actions, their views are heard and government becomes an instrument of their purposes.

To Rousseau's theory of participatory democracy, J.S. Mill and C.D.H. Cole add the context of a modern political system. Especially pertinent in our times because of the incessant business rhetoric in both govern-ment and education, Mill criticizes those who equate the business part of human affairs with the whole of the matter. In *Essays on Politics and Culture* (1963), Mill's estimation is that the business aspect of government is the least important. More fundamental is the influence of political institutions and the democratic process in promoting civic virtue.

Virtue as a quality of moral excellence in citizenship has all but disappeared in current treatises on democracy and is certainly not central to Contemporary democratic theory. According to Pratte, "Civic virtue is not a matter of mere behavior; it is a matter of forming a civic disposition, a willingness to act, in behalf of the public good while being attentive to and considerate of the feelings, needs, and attitudes of others. It implies an obligation or duty to be fair to others, to show kindness and tact, and to render agreeable service to the community" (1988, p. 17). Virtue is learned. It is the product of development and the formation of a civic conscience. Pratte refers to Green (1985) to explain that in our technological age, the actions we take as citizens in the public sphere, whether in regard to land use or solid waste disposal or any other of the myriad problems facing local communities, have enormous ramification for ourselves and generations to come. Hence civic conscience is fundamental for democratic citizens because, according to Pratte again, "It . . . promotes a civic decency. It involves behaving morally toward others as a response to their basic dignity and worth. We acknowledge our dependence on each other for the very things that we value most; human dignity and self-respect. The instrumental value of public conscience involves the recognition that behaving morally toward others enhances greater social cohesion, solidarity, and hence greater social protection than acting immorally" (p. 166).

An active, public-spirited character is best fostered, according to Mill, in a context of participatory public institutions. He maintains with Rousseau, that responsible social and political action depends largely on developing the capacity for such behavior through the educative potential of participatory democracy. In what could well pass for a stinging condemnation of the nearly exclusive focus on individual and occupational competence in the curricula of agencies serving adult learners, Mill (1963) argues that capacities for responsible public action remain undeveloped where the individual is concerned solely with his own private affairs. "The man never thinks of any collective interest, of any object to be pursued jointly with others, but only in competition with them, and in some measure at their expense" (p. 217). Later Mill argues that a man's occupational interests tend to, "Fasten his attention and interest exclusively upon himself, and upon his family as an appendage of himself;—making him indifferent to the public . . . and in his inordinate regard for his personal comforts, selfish and cowardly" (p. 230). He contends that this situation changes when the individual can participate in public affairs. His horizons are widened and the individual learns, "To weigh interests not his own; to be guided, in the case of conflicting claims, by another rule than his private partialities; to apply, at every turn, principles and maxims which have for their reason of existence the common good" (p. 217).

J.S. Mill was impressed with de Tocqueville's discussion of the dangers inherent in the development of a mass society. The sociologist C.W. Mills (1954) described threats to democracy in a mass society because only the elite express opinions and direct the thinking of everyone else. Schwertman (1958), an early adult education theorist, invoked that analysis to set forth civic education goals for adult educators—goals largely forsaken today. For J.S. Mill the best antidote to a mass society was participation in democracy at the local level by as many persons as possible.

Pateman paraphrases Mill's argument that voting every few years in national elections is of little value if citizens have not been prepared for and experienced in participation at the local level. This is especially true in large and complex societies. It is at the local level that citizens learn to govern, whether in questions about the placement of traffic signals or the preservation of land for public parks. "In other words, if individuals in a large state are to be able to participate effectively in the government of the 'great society' then the necessary qualities underlying this participation have to be fostered and developed at the local level" (Pateman, p. 31). It cannot be stressed too often that by participating in the democratic process on the smaller scale of local problems that greatly affect the quality of life and engender excitement and commitment, citizens learn how to exercise judgment and autonomy regarding national and international level issues. This is true regardless of social class. Again, Mill is instructive on this point. "It is by political discussion that the manual laborer, whose employment is a routine, and whose way of life brings him in contact with no variety of impressions, circumstances, or ideas is taught that remote causes, and events which take place far off, have a most sensible effect even on his personal interests" (1919, p. 278).

Building on the Classical theory of participatory democracy laid by Rousseau and expanded by J.S. Mill, Cole (1913; 1920) argues that people learn to participate in directing the affairs of their community through membership in organizations and associations. "Such settings are the schools of democracy, requiring the members to be self-governing, expected to participate in setting direction and decision-making, free in other words to control their own affairs. Duties and tasks are assigned to different members, power and authority are delegated among the membership in order that objectives may be effectively pursued" (1920, p. 104). The problem with representative government, according to Cole, is that it is *mis*representative. The citizen has no real choice of, or control over, his representative. The system, even at the most local level, frequently denies the right of the individual to participate.

The *Ohio Township Trustee Sourcebook* emphasizes Cole's point by reminding trustees that, "Citizens are in power on election day. In between elections, the trustees are in power, and have the laws of Ohio to support them" (1989, p. 13). Real, functional representation, on the other hand, implies "The constant participation of the ordinary man in the conduct of those parts of the structure of Society with which he is directly concerned, and which he has therefore the best chance of understanding" (Cole, 1920, p. 114).

As with Mill, Cole sees the educational function of participation as crucial. He is persuaded that it is only by participation that the individual could "learn democracy." To say that a system is democratic is to say that the citizens share in governing. For the Contemporary theorist this sharing in governing takes place at election time and the responsiveness of the system is guaranteed by the threat of removal from office. The quality of democracy is directly dependent on the qualities of its leaders and the conditions under which they operate. For Classical theorists the presuppositions and standards of citizenship are higher. Denise Thompson (1970) presents them in terms of the autonomy and improvability of citizens.

Both autonomy and improvability are reflected in the general demand on the part of Classical theorists for greater political involvement of ordinary citizens. Autonomy is a quality of those who know their own mind and act on their best judgements. In a practical sense for both elected officials and educators it implies, as Dewey (1925) suggested, asking people what they want, not telling them what they need or what is good for them. Merriam (1931), principle figure in the University of Chicago school of citizenship theorists, was committed to autonomy of ordinary citizens, especially at the local level. Merriam urged restoration of initiative and responsibility to citizens who know where the shoe pinches and what is in their best interests.

IMPLICATIONS FOR ADULT EDUCATION AGENCIES

Fortunately, there are signs of discontent with the widening gap between the formal political values undergirding American democracy and the lack of actual citizen engagement in the political system. Increasingly there are calls for a renewed sense of public virtue and civic purpose to counter the drift of Americans to become spectators instead of participants in public affairs. While it is clear in newly emerging democracies that the people must define their interests and fashion forms of government to achieve them, it is not less true that this responsibility endures throughout the life of a democracy. And if a thinking, deliberative, enlightened public is necessary to define its interests and to supply the will for political action, where and how do citizens come by this enlightenment, this learning, this thinking, this capacity to deliberate and supply moral conviction? Certainly, some information is available from radio talk shows, commercial and public television news and documentary programs, the print media, and township and city council meetings. The question is how to enrich these informal and somewhat haphazard sources of information with purposeful and systematic educational activities for adults who have the immediate responsibility as well as the rights of citizenship?

There are two good reasons for Adult Education agencies to take seriously the adult civic education imperative. First, Jefferson's concerns about the importance of an enlightened public for the vitality of a free society would logically seem to extend, if not directly pertain, to adults as well as school children. School-based civic education has been the primary vehicle for equipping Americans to understand the rights and fulfill the burdens of citizenship. However, schooling can only provide basic introductory knowledge about something that is as fluid and dynamic as citizenship in the modern world. Second, it is adults and not children who bear the burdens of citizenship, who require information about complex local and national issues from solid waste disposal to catastrophic health insurance, and who require skills and wisdom to put information to effective use.

Regrettably, however, there seem to be more reasons why civic responsibilities count for little in curriculum decisions by the many agencies serving the educational needs of adult learners. First, addressing the occupational and professional needs of learners through in-service training while ignoring the complex social choices that they face as citizens seems to reflect the orientation of Contemporary democratic theory. That is, such choices are the exclusive province of leaders who possess inside and specialized information. Second, where educational programming in political issues exists, the focus tends to be on national and international concerns rather than local choices that will directly and immediately impact the quality of life of participants. Fostering enlightened participation in the people's business is not recognized as a legitimate purpose for local adult education. Third, the difficult task of establishing criteria for desirable outcomes in adult civic education has been ignored. What would constitute acceptable, let alone exemplary, results in terms of learner competencies and dispositions? Fourth, there is considerable philosophical consistency in the presuppositions of Classical democracy and adult education. Both subscribe to the ideals of autonomy and improvability. Both accept the educative efficacy of participation. Yet a cursory review of the "Bill of Fare" offered by adult education providers in most localities reveals that the "meat and potatoes" of the curriculum does not include discussion of important and often controversial issues that citizens must decide. Fifth, mainstream adult education literature avoids engagement with the turbulent world of citizen decisions, focusing instead on such topics as adult learning theory, marketing, and adjustments needed in educational institutions in order to serve adult learners.

The inescapable conclusion is that Adult Education agencies are not making civic education a priority. Adult Educators are justifiably proud of their capacity to respond quickly to emerging educational needs. Yet throughout 1989, concluding with the Malta Conference between the leaders of the worlds two super powers in December, there was little effort on the part of Adult Education agencies to offer learning opportunities associated with the historic convulsions occurring in the communist world. Educational programs on the history and culture of countries grasping for democracy would have expanded the significance of fragmentary impressions gained from the news media. Here was an opportunity to promote a greater understanding of the citizenship demanded of those who would carve new democracies where none have existed and of Americans who will guide the worlds oldest democracy into the twenty-first century. Regrettably, during these most public displays of the challenges posed by democracy, opportunities to extract insights into the public responsibilities of citizenship from current events, history and literature were ignored. Repeatedly, educational offerings in public as well as private Adult Education agencies confirm the current American retreat to privatism.

REFERENCES

Arendt, Hannah. (1963). *On Revolution.* New York, Penguin Books.

Barber, Benjamin R. (1984). *Strong Democracy.* Berkeley, University of California Press.

Bellah, Robert and Associates. (1985). *Habits of the Heart: Individualism and Commitment in American Life.* Berkeley, University of California Press.

Berelson, B.R. and Associates. (1954). *Voting.* Chicago, University of Chicago Press.

Boyte, Harry C. (1989). *CommonWealth.* New York, The Free Press.

Broder, David. (1989). Washington Post, December 31, p. 7C.

Cole, G.D.H. (1913). *The World of Labour.* London, G. Bell & Sons.

Cole, G.D.H. (1920). *Social Theory.* London, Methuen.

Dahl, Robert A. (1956). *Preface to Democratic Theory.* Chicago, University of Chicago Press.

Dewey, John. (1925). Practical democracy. *The New Republic,* 54.

Easton, David. (1966). *A Systems Approach to Political Life.* Lafayette, Purdue University, Social Science Education Consortium, Publication 104, ED 013997.

Green, T. (1985). The formation of conscience in an age of technology. *American Journal of Education,* 94, 1–32.

Griffith, William. (1976). Adult educators and politics. *Adult Education Quarterly,* 26, 270–279.

Janowitz, Morris. (1983). *The Reconstruction of Patriotism.* Chicago, University of Chicago Press.

Matthews, David. (1989). Afterthoughts. *Kettering Review,* Fall.

Matthews, David. (1987). *The Promise of Democracy.* Dayton, Kettering Foundation.

Merriam, Charles E. (1931). *The Making of Citizens.* Chicago, University of Chicago Press.

Mezirow, Jack. (1989). Letter to members of Commission of Professors of Adult Education, September 11.

Mill, John Stuart. (1963). *Essays on Politics and Culture.* Himmelfarb, D. (Editor) New York, Macmillan.

Mills, C. Wright. (1954). *Mass Society and Liberal Education.* Notes and Essays on Education for Adults, No. 9. Chicago, Center for the Study of Liberal Education for Adults.

Ohio Township Trustee Association. (1989). *Ohio Township Trustee Sourcebook.* Columbus.

Pateman, Carole. (1970). *Participation and Democratic Theory.* Oxford, Cambridge University Press.

Pratte, Richard. (1988). *The Civic Imperative.* New York, Teachers College Press, Columbia University.

Rousseau, Jean Jacques. (1968). *The Social Contract.* Translated by M. Cranston. New York, Penguin Books.

Sartori, G. (1962). *Democratic Theory.* Detroit, Wayne State University Press.

Schumpeter, Joseph. (1943). *Capitalism, Socialism, and Democracy.* London, George Allen and Undwin.

Schwertman, John. (1958). *I Want Many Lodestars.* Notes and Essays on Education for Adults, No. 21. Chicago, Center for the Study of Liberal Education for Adults.

Stewart, David. (1982). Exploding the apolitical myth: The political dimensions of adult education. *Lifelong Learning Research Conference Proceedings,* College Park, University of Maryland.

Thompson, Dennis F. (1970). *The Democratic Citizen.* Cambridge, Cambridge University Press.

Woyach, Robert. (1989). Strengthening citizenship. *The Civic Arts Review,* Delaware, Ohio Wesleyan University, 2, Summer.

Chapter 3

ADULT EDUCATION AND SOCIAL CHANGE

> If the hope of the world
> lies in human consciousness,
> then it is obvious that intellectuals
> cannot go on forever avoiding their share
> of responsibility for the world and hiding their
> distaste for politics under an alleged need to be independent.
>
> Vaclav Havel, President
> Czechoslovak Socialist Republic
> Address to United States Congress
> February 21, 1990

In this chapter, historical examples of educational initiatives that were designed to provide adults with civic knowledge, skills, and dispositions in order to develop and implement visions of a better society will be described. Assumptions about citizenship, democracy, and the role of education in fostering social change that guided these educational programs will be identified. Also, of special interest is the question of whether the humanities were specifically utilized in these earlier educational initiatives to promote critical inquiry and discussion about the social vision sought by planners and participants. As will be further considered in Chapter 5, the humanities are potent resources for a reflective approach to life. As Peterson (1987) reports for participants in the Colloquium on the Humanities and the American People, "The importance of the humanities stems from . . . their capacity to change, elevate, and improve both the common civic life and individual lives. . . . They make possible the shared reflection, communication, and participation upon which a democratic community depends. They are the basis of reasoned civic discourse; and they are centrally concerned with the relation between the individual and the community" (p. 3).

Historically, adult civic education programs have been ephemeral, episodic, and spasmodic. Yet, the lessons learned from these initiatives are instructive for adult educators because they illustrate the perennial questions of whether and how Adult Education agencies can be part of educational efforts that combine instruction and learning with action to bring about social change. The objectives stated for such efforts were ambitious and give some indication of the rich diversity that is civic education. They included empowering the poor through increased voter registration, persuading farmers to insist that government serve their interests, helping newly enfranchised voters understand the concept of the common good as a criterion for political decisions, informing citizens about vital political, economic, and social issues, and equipping middle class citizens with the knowledge and skills necessary to carry out plans of action for social change. Since there is no precise or singular way to educate for citizenship, presumably achieving results such as those listed above suffices as evidence that civic education has occurred.

Education has always been viewed as a means to change behavior or to equip individuals with the potential to do so. In the history of education its most conventional purposes have been, and to a large extent continue to be, expressed in terms of transmitting the wisdom and values of the culture, helping learners adapt to the expectations of society at large and of employers in particular, and helping individuals adjust to the rapid pace of change by providing the skills to continue learning throughout life. It is assumed in these conventions that what is to be learned forms the basic elements of social life and is in the learner's best interests. Thus, in both schooling for youngsters and in adult education the interests of society and those of individual learners are seen as compatible. It is assumed, warns Phyllis Cunningham (1988, p. 134), "That the way the world is organized is natural and the appropriate role of educators is to use their knowledge and skills in behalf of that order."

Social change, then, is not usually embraced as an objective of educational systems. In fact, in dynamic societies, where change is the product of so many forces, it is difficult to trace the precise contribution of education to the accomplishment of change. The printing press, the telephone, and the automobile are examples of technological catalysts for massive social change. Wars, revolutions, religious fervor, and natural disasters have also been instrumental in precipitating change in the organization and structure of societies. Historically, education has been employed as the principal tool to ensure that the changes in society orchestrated by inventors, statesmen, generals, clerics, industrialists, revolutionaries, and others endure. For example, in colonial times sons of wealthy Americans were encouraged to obtain their education in this

country rather than travel to England or Europe for it. Those who chose
to seek their education abroad were barred from holding public office for
a period of time so that their loyalty to the republic and lack of contami-
nation by royalist ideas could be ascertained. Today, it is widely accepted
that no nation can maintain itself without an effective program of civic
education. In free societies, schools seek to transmit and perpetuate the
principles and values of democracy through the civics curriculum.

There have been instances, however, when existing educational systems were modified or new ones deliberately created as vehicles to
facilitate fundamental social change. The Morrill Act signed by President Abraham Lincoln in 1862 to establish new land-grant colleges to
provide a practical education for the sons and daughters of merchants,
farmers, and tradesmen is an example. The legislation was not a product
of pressure from the higher education community which, for the most
part, was content to continue indefinitely with the existing system. Rather
it resulted from months and years of ferment and pressure by ordinary
citizens who organized themselves in agricultural and commercial societies to demand a new form of education. Following the Soviet Union's
successful launching of Sputnik in 1957, the ensuing public alarm over
this technological achievement by its adversaries resulted in American
schools placing new emphasis on science and mathematics in order to
keep the United States competitive. More recently, the United States
Congress, and ultimately the judiciary system, have required changes in
school curricula in response to citizen concerns about what children
learn regarding race and gender.

In adult education literature, no other issue has produced as many
intellectual contortions as the question of the appropriate relationship
between adult education and social change. The premise advanced here
is that adult civic education is pivotal to accomplishing the changes in
structure and behavior that society, through its public dialogue over
such questions, decides are desirable. Seeking social change through
civic education is predicated on a vision of a better world. The vision is
rarely held in pacific possession and public dialogue about it is often
contentious, involving diverse opinions, values, and conflicting interpretations of data. The humanities provide insights and perspective regarding this diversity. As an instrument of social change, education is sometimes the subject of the dialogue and, always a prerequisite to participate
intelligently and effectively.

THE CONCEPTUAL LEGACY

Some American adult education philosophers in the 1920s and 1930s were struck by the promise they saw in its capacity to formulate and contribute to a vision of a better world. Their convictions have contributed to conceptual and programmatic legacies that forge a link between adult education and democracy by improving the capacity of learners to function effectively as citizens. Social change was not accepted as a legitimate objective of adult education among all those who were grappling after the World War I with the question of *what kind of education adults needed.* Stubblefied (1988) identifies three groups of theorists who gave thoughtful consideration to the question.

One group focused on the diffusion of knowledge and culture, interrelating life and scholarship in order to improve life and the general state of culture in America. In their view adult education was an instrument of intellectual improvement but without an agenda for social reform or change. James Harvey Robinson and other founders of the New School for Social Research, and persons associated with the Carnegie Corporation's support for adult education such as Morse A. Cortwright are representative of the first group. In *Adult Education,* the first textbook of adult education, Lyman Bryson (1936) included political education in his classification scheme of five principle functions. Civic knowledge was included as part of remedial education, along with homemaking and child care. While Rachal (1989) says that Bryson interpreted political education to mean not only recognition or understanding of political concerns, but action and advocacy regarding them, Stubblefield disagrees. Rather, he maintains that Bryson believed that adult education, "Could best serve social ends as an instrument of intellectual empowerment and not in directing social change" (p. 47). The distinction between acquiring knowledge and acting on it continues to be troublesome for contemporary adult education scholars.

A second group gave preeminence to liberal education as a vehicle to foster rationality and growth in understanding, insight, and wisdom through provision of high culture for the masses. Education was not designed to provide vocational skills. Rather, its worth was intrinsic. Their fundamental premises were that liberally educated adults form their own opinions and are not led by the crowd, examine the presuppositions in others' arguments, tolerate differences of opinion, and appreciate human worth. Such persons have mastered the intellectual requirements of citizenship. Whether and how this learning results in and is enhanced by participation in civic affairs is not the educator's concern. Everett Dean Martin, Robert M. Hutchins, Mortimer Adler, Alexander Meiklejohn, and John Walker Powell are representative of this school of thought.

The third group, including Joseph K. Hart, Eduard C. Lindeman, and Harry Overstreet, derived the unifying principle of adult education from social purposes. For Hart (1937), democracy, education, and social purposes were all intertwined. "A democracy is not a social order . . . it is an *endurable social disorder* within which education is going on; within which men and women of goodwill and growing intelligence are trying to discover for themselves and their neighbors the ever more satisfying moral and spiritual goods of human living. . . . Our disorders, our conflicts, our problems, even our contradictions are the most fertile soils for the growth of critical understanding and self-government." According to Lindeman (1926), "Adult education will become an agency of progress if its short-time goal of self-improvement can be made compatible with a long-time, experimental but resolute policy of changing the social order" (p. 104). Progress, in other words, occurs when learners immersed in community problems apply civic learning to their resolution. According to Brookfield (1984), Lindeman argued firmly and unequivocally that, "The goals of adult education were social in nature, and in its fostering of democratic habits of thought and action, adult education was a major force set against demagoguery, prejudice, and dictatorship" (p. 195).

Scholars in this third group adopted the premise that adult education is one of the means by which people learn the meaning of democracy, and that given the dynamic evolving society of which it is a part, adult education cannot help but be concerned with social change. The legacy of adult education as an instrument of social change, as documented by Stubblefield, remains incomplete and inconsistent. The divisions within this first generation of theorists presaged a contemporary schism regarding the purposes of adult civic education. Should Adult Education agencies assist people who seek civic knowledge and skills in order to implement their vision of a better society, providing order and synthesis and direction to the learning which accrues from such involvement? Or, are skillful applications of civic knowledge essentially political purposes and activities and hence to be avoided by educators at all cost?

Some contemporary authors, such as Rachal (1989) and Cunningham (1988), take the position that as a source of power, knowledge acquired through participation in adult education can be used to promote conformity and protect the status quo. They maintain, however, that in a democratic society knowledge can and should be used to empower, to enhance the voice of learners in matters of local or national or international concern. In fact, if necessary, adult education should even play a subversive role for planning and directing desired change.

Other authors (Sheets, Jayne, & Spence 1953; Apps, 1979; Darkenwald & Merriam, 1982; Brookfield, 1986) and most adult education practitioners, are ambivalent about the relationship between education and action. They attempt to resolve the question by distinguishing between adult education for social change and education for civic competence. They reason that sponsoring adult education to help citizens develop skills in using information to achieve social purposes is an inescapably political activity. Since such education threatens established interests it is more appropriately undertaken by the mass media. As an appropriate function for Adult Education agencies it is suspect. Education for civic competence, on the other hand, is an aspect of literacy involving facts about government, citizen rights, and individual responsibility to make informed voter judgments. It is part of the civics curriculum, a distinct, academically respectable, and nonthreatening content area for adult education that can be packaged and presented to individual learners who have nothing in common but their enrollment in a particular course.

This facile distinction between adult education for social change and for civic competence is as sterile as it is convenient. What would an analysis of the actual civic education available from Adult Education agencies reveal about the state of citizenship in the United States? Would it reveal any vision of the kind of society that adult educators want to promote in the next century? The distinction permits a pretense of concern with community problems to be maintained, while freeing Adult Education agencies from involvement in the potential for contention contained in those problems. Yet, it leaves several civic education issues unresolved.

First, the motivation for acquiring civic knowledge is usually related to making judgements and taking action about some specific problem and such problems often involve controversy. Problems are suitable grist for the mill in every facet of adult education but this one. Yet, the knowledge and skills necessary to force a nursing home to comply with government health standards, or to persuade a local industry to improve

its waste disposal practices, or to formulate and present land use proposals to a township zoning commission involve a vision for the future
and constitute in part what it means to have civic competence.

Second, most Americans who have already completed a civics course
in school are hardly motivated to seek additional civic knowledge and
skills from an Adult Education agency. It is as though both learners and
educators conspire to agree that lifelong learning is important in all
spheres of life but this one. Possibilities for integrating civic education
into other established adult education curriculum areas are not discussed.
Differences in need for civic education on the part of those becoming
citizens and those already possessing citizenship are not considered.

Third, civic competence is a dynamic and evolving phenomenon. It is
part of the experience of living in a community. It cannot be learned in a
vacuum, in isolation from public problems. Nor can civic education be
antiseptically packaged in a course and uncontaminated by value judgements that accompany those problems.

Fourth, learners seeking civic knowledge and skills in order to influence public decisions regarding a specific issue present themselves in
groups, with definite opinions about the problem they are studying and
convictions, albeit prematurely formed, about how it should be resolved.
Their discourse swirls and buzzes. The purposes of adult education,
however, are usually defined in terms of addressing the deficiencies of
individuals. It is educators who do the assessing and such assessments of
learning needs are denuded of references to values. Groups are a less
tidy constituency for education. They wear their values on their sleeves
and are not impressed with so-called academic objectivity.

Fifth, the distinction between education for social change and education for civic competence clouds the difference between promoting learning in relation to a problem and promoting or advocating specific
positions or solutions. Adult Education agencies can and should be
advocates, but only for thorough, disciplined, and balanced understanding of public problems. Such understanding includes consideration of
alternative solutions. It is the stuff of adult civic education. Adult educators are advocates in the sense that citizens start with a deficit of information and knowledge and stand to benefit from the assistance of educators
in accomplishing the difficult task of educating themselves and their
fellow citizens. Citizens also learn from guided reflection on the lessons
of experience and implications of that experience for resolution of
future public issues.

THE CULTURE OF DEMOCRACY

Adult education scholars such as Thomas and Harris-Jenkins (1975), Fletcher (1980), and Lovett (1983) consider the involvement of Adult Education agencies in citizen learning and action regarding societal problems an act of creation of culture, what humanists such as Catharine R. Stimpson (1988) refer to as a "culture of democracy, a republic of discourse." If, indeed, a major purpose of adult civic education is to assist people in identifying, articulating, and solving public problems, then in doing so it is an agent in the creation of culture. Fletcher describes culture as an active, shared component of life. It does not exist independently of its creators and its creation depends very much upon the problems people face. He argues that any social system or organization such as adult education which can ignore the troubles, dilemmas, and choices of its community is not part of that community. "For adult education should be put to work at the point where people are creating the type of community in which they want to live—where they are improving their own conditions together" (p. 68). In this manner it is an agent in the creation of culture, a proper vehicle for civic education, and as such cannot be separated from the purpose of improving society. Social change, predicated on some vision of a better society, fundamentally involves the political condition. It is a civic matter requiring dialogue and choice in matters where value differences and uncertainty are endemic.

The culture and identity of American society, unlike Europe, is not derived from centuries of traditions based on class and passed down through generations, but rather from certain political principles that were adopted and articulated in its founding documents. Peterson (1987) maintains that these principles of freedom, equality, and self-government can only be made relevant to modern realities and problems by a reflective people. There is nothing about democracy that guarantees protection from falling prey to demagoguery and slogans. Rather, the mindless television sitcoms, soap operas, romance novels, and sporting events so prevalent in American society are antithetical to the reflection that must precede intelligent civic discourse, the lifeblood of a democracy. The culture of democracy falters when public understanding of and participation in public issues is dulled by passivity and flaccidity, consequences of a lack of civic education.

The task, as Pratte (1988) says, of establishing a democratic civic culture of informed, active, knowledgeable, and ethically obligated citizens is a formidable one. Citizen participation in governance is a vital part of such a culture. Historically, adult education initiatives have been instrumental in revitalizing citizen participation in public issues, and hence the culture of democracy itself. For this reason, those initiatives warrant careful consideration.

THE PROGRAMMATIC LEGACY

In 1951, Trustees of the Emil Schwarzhaupt Foundation established, in concert with the Division of Social Studies of the University of Chicago, a Committee on Education for American Citizenship. The purpose was to provide guidance to the Foundation in carrying out its mandate to promote better citizenship. Carl Tjerandsen (1980) relates that the Committee identified some unfortunate consequences of the growing sentiment that citizens are unable to influence their government, regardless of level, in any meaningful way. "They no longer have a feeling of belonging to a community ... problems are just too big or change too swiftly for their efforts to matter. ... Those who have a private interest at stake will tend to be the more active participants. ... There is an increasing tendency on the part of many to grasp at simplistic solutions which turn out to be inappropriate to the problems" (p. 11). The resulting apathy or withdrawal results in low voter turnout, especially in local elections, the tendency to defer to experts on complex questions, and substantial skepticism about government agencies and officials. These conditions are especially dangerous for a democratic society that is built on the assumption that ultimate responsibility and authority for public affairs is vested in citizens.

Historically, programs of adult civic education were initiated in response to feelings of apathy and conditions of powerlessness that are deleterious to democracy. Some of these programs have been selected to be reviewed here. The purpose is not to evaluate these programs, nor to examine their inner workings, nor even to identify the factors that contributed to their successes and failures. Rather, they are presented to illustrate a legacy that has nearly vanished from contemporary adult education. In relating adult civic learning to specific public issues, they suggest approaches to combining learning with acting—a dichotomy that today so immobilizes and detracts from the ability of adult educators to significantly influence social change. In every instance, these programs embody the courage, charisma, and contributions of significant adult educators. Furthermore, the characteristics of these programs stand in sharp contrast to the school-based civics education curriculum.

The Southern Farmers Alliance

Theodore Mitchell's (1987) *Political education in the southern farmers' alliance: 1887–1900* is an account of an adult education agency organized by farmers to address their changing economic and political conditions after the Civil War. In reviewing the book, Stubblefield (1989) suggests that it offers some challenges to andragogical dogma, in that the educators were more than process facilitators: "they took positions, they taught, and they advocated." The Alliance used adult civic education intentionally as a central strategy in challenges to the dominant culture. A fundamental problem for the Alliance leadership was to legitimize social activism in the minds of learners who had learned and internalized deference. Both Mitchell's book and the story it relates have importance that transcends the experience of southern farmers in the late nineteenth century.

Leaders in the Alliance movement claimed that it had done more to educate the great mass of people in the principles of government and the rights and duties of citizenship than all the schools ever had. Its importance, Mitchell says is that it, "Broadened the scope of political discourse in ways that still demand attention" (p. 4). It did so by engaging its nearly one million members across the South in a program of political education that drew ordinary farmers and merchants into the political debate over government support of railroads and industries seeking to take advantage of abundant cotton, coal, and timber. Through a systematic educational program Alliance educators encouraged common people to insist that government serve the interests of the small independent producer. Through education the Alliance strove to change the relationship between its members and their elected officials by gaining power over their government and its laws.

In this case, civic education meant several things: (1) understanding what had happened in the political economy to change the nature of agriculture as an enterprise; (2) participation in a culture (a culture of democracy) consciously fashioned by the movement to teach people about cooperation and mutual improvement, to change their isolation from one another and improve their social condition, to increase their social pleasure, and promote confidence in and friendship for one another; (3) recognition of their commonality of circumstance and identity of interests; (4) demystifying politics and giving farmers basic intellectual tools, such as literacy and numeracy in the context of building skills in political analysis; and (5) encouraging education itself, but also critiquing public school education in order to promote a curriculum that empowered farmers and laborers and their children.

Alliance leaders maintained that farmers learned best from their straitened circumstances, that experience was the best teacher, but that experience also taught farmers that they needed to know more. "Some came on horseback, some on foot. Families loaded on wagons trundled slowly along the road in the early morning hours. Some five hundred strong, men, women, and children, black and white, headed toward the church at the crossroads town of Shady Grove, Georgia ... to take part in the Alliance Rally" (p. 48). In Georgia they were called *rallies, gatherings* in Virginia, *camps* in Texas. They gathered for a day of respite from toil, for socializing, playing, eating, and political educating. The meetings generated a sense of identity and connections with the outside world. Often the meetings were pageants for the community as a whole. Singing was a large part of the cultural experience, an educational tool in itself. Songs were followed by speeches, and then eating. Ideas were presented by speakers, countered by others, discussed over meals, and refined or altered later in the afternoon. The format encouraged participation. Presentations and discussions of the ills facing farmers were followed by organizational sessions on how to put the ideas that were learned to work.

Encouraging members to accept political responsibility despite inhibitions caused by custom, myth, and negative self-perception was the paramount educational objective. Farmers were inclined to separate politics from economics and, in the political realm, to put themselves in the hands of professional politicians and the social elite. Burdened by illiteracy, isolated from centers of commerce and political discourse, and bound by cultural traditions that militated against independent political action, the average farmer was ill equipped to exert influence on the political order. Politicians encouraged the citizen passivity and deference to leaders associated with what is now called the "contemporary theory of democracy" as discussed in Chapter 2.

Alliance leaders promoted, in the face of the inertia of tradition, a sense of self-determination and power to make history. They utilized the humanities tradition of songs, stories, and historical parallels drawn between their own circumstances and those of agrarians in Greece, France, and Ireland in order to drive home lessons about taking responsibility for one's own affairs. From the study of history farmers obtained a liberating perspective on current events. The plight of Russian serfs illustrated the futility of doing nothing when rights are restricted. English peasants, on the other hand, were slowly achieving reforms through peaceful means. Education, then, was the key to securing reform. Not only kings and presidents, but peasants and workers could make history. It was a lesson to be repeated later in other adult civic education programs.

The National League of Women Voters

Sara Brumbaugh (1946) reports in *Democratic Experience and Education in the National League of Women Voters* that the League's purposes were closely related to women's suffrage. Newly enfranchised women needed disinterested or unbiased information when confronted with a bewildering array of citizen choices related to postwar problems in 1920. Who could provide it? The political parties were partisan, more interested in candidates than issues, and in winning elections than in developing public intelligence. Public schools then, as now, were only interested in children. No other structure appeared on the horizon to do the job. And while the task of developing understanding and judgement of citizens to vote was at first thought to be temporary, the League soon learned that education by and for participation in government must be continuous. Fresh from the suffrage movement in which education gave direction to social change, pioneer League members set about to create an organization and a process of education that would overcome any barriers to the understanding and full, free communication that democracy requires. To the League, civic education consisted of, "Experiencing a relation to government and acquiring information and capacity to act in that relation in the public interest" (p. 65).

At its first national convention in Cleveland in 1921, the League came face to face with the perennial problems that confront any Adult Education agency conducting civic education: How to be at the same time democratic as well as efficient in the promotion of civic education? How to avoid being taken over by special interests? How to move from study to action, that is, how to give effect politically to opinions formed on the basis of knowledge and thought? At first, the League thought that it had twin objectives, education of voters and promotion of good government by lobbying for the issues and positions it supported. It soon discovered that participation in political activity had great educational value, or to put it another way, civic education occurs through active participation in government. Gradually, after noting the unusual quality of educational result produced by preparation for and engagement in political action, the League came to place stronger faith in and emphasis upon the educative nature of activity. At the same time, it was generally recognized that there is more to civic education than political activity.

The League has consistently placed its main reliance for civic education upon full and free sharing of insights. Brumbaugh quotes an early League publication concerning this issue: "To talk freely and frankly is the chief reason for . . . [League] meetings; to talk until we come to using the same terms with the same meaning" (p. 25). But debate, as Brumbaugh notes, was not part of discussion. "It is assumed that the objective is not to determine whether a preconceived course is right or wrong, but to study . . . in order to get as full an understanding as possible of the various factors involved, the values at stake, and the possibilities open, as a basis of common agreement upon a tentative plan for meeting a confronting difficulty" (p. 25). In time, the League came to focus its adult education efforts on a few central themes that represented the problems in which the majority of members had interest. The source of program ideas has always been the members' interests and experiences.

The need to be impartial and the importance of taking action are closely related. Those adversely affected by the League's long intensive lobbying campaign to extend the civil service system and eliminate patronage from government service, complained loudly about propaganda and partisanship. League leaders came to the position that it was their responsibility to turn the intelligence generated through education into legislative power. It seemed to them lamentably ineffective to be spending precious time in study while self-seeking interests were mobilizing pressures upon government. There is no point in amassing knowledge unless it is spread to more people and moves them to use their knowledge effectively. By constantly focusing its own and the public's attention on the common good the League attempted to counter the growing power of special interests. "There are questions well known to members of the League which transcend all party lines. . . . Action may be required . . . when partisan groups hesitate and the general public is tired" (p. 64). By maintaining a nonpartisan posture the League has been able to share its hard-won knowledge with the public-at-large and thus pave the way for thoughtful decisions which all citizens are called upon to make.

Concern for the public interest means acting in the public interest while adhering to a nonpartisan line of conduct. Early in its history the League stressed voting, and getting out the vote as its primary form of action. In time it began to recognize that people need to be knowledgeable about political affairs, to learn about their dependence upon them and how to deal with them effectively. Voting means something only if the issues involved are understood and have personal significance. As an agent of adult civic education, the League is interested in and gives publicity to the qualifications of candidates for public office, particularly the views of policy-forming officials. It supports and may initiate legislative measures which, after careful study, the group has approved. It keeps the spotlight primarily on political policies, needs, and developments; secondarily, on persons and agencies. The League demonstrates to other Adult Education agencies that study and action regarding the functions of government are defensible as legitimate educational purposes in a democracy.

Highlander Folk School

Frank Adams (1972) describes the purpose of what is now called Highlander Research and Education Center, as an adult residential center in the South for the development of community leaders among school, church, civic, labor, and farm groups, and for liberal education. Founded by Myles Horton in 1932 at Monteagle, Tennessee, and serving a variety of constituencies since then, its focus, says Tjerandsen (1980), has been "Helping people, especially the socially and economically deprived, learn to deal with problems too difficult for individuals to solve without help from their fellows" (p. 139). Early efforts to send small groups of staff members from Highlander into communities in Alabama and Tennessee in order to work with people, who it was hoped would buy into the notion that their community could be improved, did not work. It became obvious that a project could not be 'cooked up' for a community. There needed to be a sense of a problem that called for new thinking. Reflecting on these incidents, Horton recognized that they failed because "We were trying to create something to respond to."

Adams writes (p. 500) that from early exposure to theologian Reinhold

Niebuhr, sociologist Robert Park, educators in the Danish folk schools, and the works of Lindeman, Hart, and John Dewey, Horton learned several things that radically altered his notions of education. About community problems, he learned that involvement in a situation is vital to understanding it; that social change arises from situations in which people confront problems and look for solutions; that education in the humanities is an aid to liberating people from ignorance and poverty. About people, Horton learned to respect their ideas even though they had little education; that they could identify their problems and that they knew the answers to them. About educators, Horton learned that their job is to get people talking about their problems; to get behind their judgments and help them act and speak for themselves; to raise and sharpen questions, and to trust people to come up with the answers.

These insights led him to establish a new kind of school—not a school for teaching reading, writing, and arithmetic, but a school for problems. His goal, however, was not to solve a community problem, but it was to help individuals develop abilities to work together to solve the problem. Problems addressed through Highlander's residential workshops, always conducted on an interracial basis, have included rural health, voter registration, school desegregation, and community leader training.

Horton distinguished between dealing with what *is* and with what *ought to be.* Tjerandsen writes that Horton recognized that what was significant and unique about Highlander was, "Not that they taught people to write checks or to register to vote or even to read and write. These were part of the world that *is* and they might be useful and good things. But one could learn to write for the purpose of forging a check. What was needed was the concept of what *ought to be* —human brotherhood, dignity and democracy" (p. 142). It was not poverty that was the great problem, but rather meanness, prejudice, and tradition. This vision of a better society and the mutual solidarity among participants that would be required to bring it about were often expressed through music. Horton, Adams says, found that, "Song and dance sparked people with determination and self-assurance in ways that no other communication could" (p. 508).

Grants from the Emil Schwarzhaupt Foundation in 1953, 1956, and 1961 enabled Highlander to give primary emphasis to the development of civic knowledge and power. Reviewers of Horton's initial proposal wrote: "In our opinion, Highlander Folk School is in a position to make a real contribution to the furthering of democratic purposes in

the South. Its leadership is indigenous to the South. . . . The South faces
serious problems of land use, education, health, housing, etc. To cope
with these the improvement of citizen participation is vital. Basic to
improvement of such participation is the training of leadership." (Recommendations to the trustees of the ESF from the Committee on Education
for American Citizenship of the University of Chicago, April 27, 1953,
pp. 41–42, ESF files.)

Nowhere was this potential to make a difference in society that the
Foundation envisioned for Highlander more evident than in the citizenship schools on Sea Island, South Carolina. Horton's hopes for what
leadership training might become were not realized until he got involved
with the problems of Johns Island.

South Carolina Sea Island Citizenship Schools

Johns Island, adjacent to the city of Charleston, is the largest of a chain
known as the Sea Islands. A majority of the residents in the early 1950s
were black. Many owned small farms. Others fished for a living or
worked in Charleston. Isolation from the mainland for decades created a
society with poor education, poor health care, and little economic
opportunity. Sandra Oldendorf (1987) says that devices such as the grand-
father clause, the white primary, the poll tax, and the literacy test which
kept southern politics free of black influence, were operative here as
well. Few blacks were registered to vote. In 1954 Septima Clark, a former
teacher from Johns Island who had joined the staff at Highlander,
invited a local black leader from the Island, Esau Jenkins, to attend a
Highlander workshop. Afterwards, Jenkins asked Horton to help him
establish schools to teach adults to read and write in order to vote. Out of
this invitation the Citizenship Schools began.

Horton's purpose in the Sea Islands, according to Herman Blake (1969),
was very simple. "He wanted to develop the leadership in the rural
South through a process of getting the folk to articulate their problems as they saw them and then develop indigenous programs to attack
those problems. . . . Such efforts, however, were to come only after the
grassroots residents of a particular community had requested the as—
sistance of the Highlander Folk School" (quoted in Tjerandsen, p. 143).
So while the initial work on Johns Island would involve teaching reading, writing, and arithmetic, the three R's became a *means* to the development of effective citizens, a central concern of Highlander. "We

are getting results," Horton said, "not only in terms of reading and writing but in terms of intelligent first-class citizens—hundreds and hundreds of them—simply because we began by assuming that they *could* be citizens" (Tjerandsen, p. 143).

Success on the Sea Islands led ultimately to a citizenship education program throughout the South under the aegis of the Southern Christian Leadership Conference and other civil rights organizations. Eventually the lessons learned in the Sea Islands were applied over a 600-mile radius. Highlander workshops were providing down-to-earth practical training in the meaning and practice of citizenship for thousands of persons. It is important to note, however, that the program grew not only geographically but also in sophistication—from voter registration to participation in precinct and party activity, to concern with qualifications of candidates, to gaining access to boards of voluntary community organizations, to becoming informed on issues through learning to read newspapers critically.

In analyzing adult educator philosophy and goals for public affairs or civic education programs, Jimmerson, Hastay, and Long (1989) suggest two categories. Some educators seek revolutionary purposes in terms of a major change in the structure of society. They place Myles Horton in this category. Others, whom these authors call functionalists, assume that structures of society are basically sound but that citizens need training to use the system better. Consider the contributions to civic competence that resulted from the Sea Islands project. How a free society can sustain revolutionary behavior such as this, and still survive, is difficult to imagine. Tjerandsen's description of these outcomes is paraphrased as follows:

1. Attitudes were changed. Hopes were encouraged that one's lot could be improved by working with others. Many were helped to gain a sense of being somebody, a necessary forerunner to achieving a sense of first-class citizenship.
2. Learning to read and write opened the door to communication throughout the whole world of the written word. Special attention was given to skills needed to read a newspaper critically.
3. Understanding government structure and procedures, the political process and the strategy and tactics of political action were emphasized. Blacks were taught how to discover and demand the public services which were available to white citizens.

4. Community leaders learned how to conduct meetings so as to develop understanding and make decisions, how to role-play to gain insight, how to involve other residents in community activity, how to organize voter registration campaigns, and how to form organizations for community betterment.

5. The lecture was rejected as a teaching method in favor of exploring the connection between the life experiences of the students and the various problems they faced at the community level.

6. Thousands of new leaders, the more and the less sophisticated, urban and rural, educated and uneducated, were able to join together in a cause and to work to improve the welfare of all.

7. Participants developed a willingness to commit themselves to help others in their communities.

8. Blacks gained the courage and the skills needed to run for office and were elected in growing numbers.

9. Many blacks prepared themselves for effective membership in the network of committees and boards through which so many public functions are conducted.

Public Issue Forums

Leonard P. Oliver (1983; 1987) has traced the evolution of the public forum concept and practice in the United States from the colonial period to modern times. In *Study Circles,* Oliver writes that religious, civic, and intellectual leaders have arisen periodically to create structures and movements to encourage public discussion of the important issues of the day. The public issue movement, prompted by varying conditions in our national life, has taken many forms, has had great diversity in local sponsorship, and has had a shelf-life lasting from one to forty years. The underlying premise of all such programs has been the conviction that every adult has an important contribution to make to public life beyond the voting booth. David Matthews, Kettering Foundation President, writes in the Foreword to Oliver's *The Art of Citizenship,* that public issue discussion programs have one feature in common. "They are attempts . . . to make democracy work more effectively through the informed, intelligent participation of those most directly affected by public policy decisions— the local citizen" (p. 4). The programs vary, however, on the strength of the link established between citizens and policy makers, or to put it another way, on the relationship of citizen discussion to practical affairs or sociopolitical change. It is the perennial dichotomy between knowledge and action that has divided adult education theorists and practitioners.

Some public forum programs have encouraged broad public participation as an end itself. That is, the goal is that adult civic learning experiences will encourage concerned citizens to develop knowledge of public issues as well as habits, skills, and competencies that are necessary for living in a democratic society. This was the philosophy behind the Studebaker Forums that were initiated in 1932 through the Des Moines public school system, and later expanded into a national program that lasted until 1940. John Studebaker (1935) argued that it is futile to expect much progress in solving our perplexing national problems so long as the understanding of them rests upon the flimsy background of civic knowledge acquired in school. "Educators cannot crowd into that brief period all the knowledge, ideals, habits, sense of civic responsibility, and familiarity with the right use of governmental machinery that adults must now possess as a proper equipment for life in a modern democracy" (P. 16). Nor, he argued, could people with a college education be expected to supply the necessary "leaven in the lump" of civic ignorance and irresponsibility. Rather, the key to solving society's greatest ills was adult civic literacy that is stimulated by discussion in a community-wide, and eventually nationwide, system of public forums.

The program became a nation-wide phenomenon when Studebaker became U.S. Commissioner of Education in 1934. Oliver (1983) notes that this marked the first time the federal government devoted sizeable resources to a national program with the sole objective of enhancing adult civic education. Especially relevant to the discussion here is that the forums, both in Des Moines and nationally, were deliberately designed *not* to result in any action. In Studebaker's words: "The function of the public forum is to *educate*, not to promote any particular program of action. Of action and pressure groups we have plenty in which citizens may work for whatever Utopias they choose; but of educational machinery we have little enough and that little must not be prostituted to other purposes than the exchange of ideas and points of view, the development of tolerance and open-mindedness, and the encouragement of habits of critical thinking" (p. 75). These qualities of tolerance, open-mindedness, and habits of critical thinking amount to a kind of civic virtue that operates at its best when citizens are able to probe partisan positions with cold objective logic. Contrast this understanding with Pratte's (1988) view that civic virtue includes a willingness to act in behalf of the public good.

Studebaker reflected the common American faith, embraced and promulgated by many adult educators, that as access to essential information and engagement in debate about public issues increases, the more likely the government will make wise decisions. Citizen education was the end sought. Oliver says that this and other programs of public discussion, such as the 1935–1940 United States Department of Agriculture "Schools of Philosophy" for Farmers and Farmer Discussion Groups, the 1975–1976 American Issues Forum, and the 1980 American Association of Community and Junior Colleges' National Energy Forum, did not have social and political change as an objective; what participants did with the knowledge and skills was up to them. Nor were there any mechanisms built in to assess participant opinions on the issues or to communicate the results to policy-makers. These programs seem to reflect the view found in contemporary democratic theory that the role of citizens is to choose its leaders wisely by being informed of their views on the issues. Governing and policy making, however, is left up to elected leaders.

Other public issue discussion programs did seek to initiate thoughtful action that would have impact on government decisions. Oliver documents a philosophy that citizen education, through public forums, can have both individual learning goals and serve as instrumentalities, or "means" as well for citizen participation in governance, to influence public policy. Relying less on faith that civic knowledge alone will produce good government, these programs have struggled with the question of how to use public forums to create an informed, active, and involved citizenry that would be the vehicle for social and political transformation.

Remarkably, programs with expectations that participants will not only learn but also engage in efforts to influence public decisions have endured and appear to be flourishing. The Great Decisions program, sponsored by the Foreign Policy Association, was created in 1955. Oliver (1983) says it has managed to remain vital for several reasons: timeliness and importance of issues, impressive educational materials, nonpartisanship, openness to a variety of sponsors or hosts, and the opportunity it affords for citizens to both express their views and to have those views receive a hearing at the highest policy levels of government.

Other programs have strengthened the linkage between participants and policy makers in a variety of ways. Oliver presents case studies of citizen leagues in Minneapolis-St. Paul, Jacksonville (Florida), and Syracuse that conduct research and education on pressing policy issues and then work for eventual integration of their findings into public policy. The Minneapolis League takes the posture that it is, "A consultant to the community, an agenda-setting organization ... providing in-depth analysis and discussion of issues and alternatives before they reach crisis levels" (1983, p. 24). A new zoo, a state university for older students, a public-private sharing of medical facilities, and a master plan for center-city revitalization are examples of the fruits of its orientation that combines education and consensus-building with action. Minneapolis League members work at monitoring progress on its recommendations. Clearly, the classical theory of democracy, with citizens seeking rough epistemological parity with public officials, underlies the behavior of League members.

The Domestic Policy Association's National Issues Forum, established in 1982, conducts annual policy briefings with public officials in a variety of formats, including teleconference "downlinks" with communities around the country. Oliver says that the DPA seeks to be an activist force through discussion of the issues between participants and public and private sector leaders. The DPA forums attempt to bridge the chasm between citizens and elected officials. They provide opportunities for citizens to both systematically learn and be heard.

In the final analysis, assumptions that adults have about citizenship, including their rights and their obligations toward the commonwealth, are affected by the introduction to civics and government that was provided in school. Adult experience augments this instruction. No democratic nation can solve its problems and exercise world leadership unless its citizens possess civic competence. It is therefore, important to briefly review the evolution of civic education as it is presented to school children. The assumption is that education for citizenship is a lifelong endeavor, and while there are many sources of civic education, the school provides a base on which to build.

CIVIC EDUCATION FOR YOUTH

In every age the role of citizen has had a variety of meanings and been a subject of continuous debate. In tracing its evolution from the Greek city-states to the present day, citizenship theorists such as Morris Janowitz (1983) and N. Freeman Butts (1989) make it clear that what it means to be citizen and what is required of the citizen mirrors political, economic, and social conditions. Historically, schools have been the primary agents of civic education. It might be assumed that the goal in Social Studies, Civics, and Government courses would be that children, adolescents, and college students will learn to play their parts as informed, responsible, committed members of a modern democratic political system. It might also be assumed that the curriculum should include elements as diverse as political values, knowledge, and the skills of participation needed for making deliberate choices among real alternatives. Yet, while no idea attracts pieties as does citizenship, the goals of school-based civic education have never been entirely agreed upon.

Pratte (1988) suggests that several interpretations of goals exist. "For some, civic education is the teaching of civic knowledge and skills—a civic literacy. Students learn the rights and duties of citizenship as a mere academic matter and keep politics and morality at arm's length" (p. 3). This is the position taken by Edward Hirsch (1987). He stresses civic literacy as the major purpose of school-based civic education, citing as an underlying premise that, "People in a democracy can be entrusted to decide all important matters for themselves because they can deliberate and communicate with one another. Persons, on the other hand, who lack civic literacy or have semiliteracy are condemned to the powerlessness of incomprehension. Knowing that they do not understand the issues and feeling prey to manipulative oversimplifications, they do not trust the system of which they are supposed to be masters. They do not feel themselves to be active participants in our republic, and they often do not vote. True enfranchisement depends upon knowledge, and knowledge upon civic literacy" (p. 12). Hirsch would acquaint all Americans with a common fund of knowledge, a common vocabulary, such as may be necessary for entrance into public dialogue. He claims that the lack of this fund of knowledge tends to keep some individuals and groups from effective participation in society.

For others, Pratte says, "The function of civic education is shaped by the fact that the public school is expected to produce citizens possessed of a national loyalty, a sense of obligation to country, a strong desire to serve it honorably, prepared, when necessary, to die in its defense" (p. 3). Pratte is concerned, however, with the danger in emphasizing patriotism that is too often synonymous with contempt for other countries, admiration for the most bloodthirsty national heroes, and suppression of efforts by groups within the nation to exercise the right of self-determination.

Others, such as Kenneth Langton and M. Kent Jennings (1968), contend that the schools should do it all. That is, civic courses should increase the student's knowledge about political institutions and processes, make him a more interested and loyal citizen, increase his understanding of his own rights and the civil rights of others, and encourage his political participation. The only area of disagreement, they maintain, is how much stress schools should give to civic education. In part, the lack of clarity with regard to scope, domain, and goals for school-based citizenship education and the diverse opinions about how much it should be emphasized may be due to the shifting and evolving nature of what it means to be a citizen in a complex technological society. In part it may also be a result of the difficulty in determining what is appropriate for young students to learn and what is better understood by adults. Whatever the reasons, it is clear from the poor showings by citizens on surveys of knowledge of public affairs and governmental structures that the majority of adults are products of civic education that is ineffective. Janowitz (1983) says that the deterioration in civic education has been occurring since 1945.

At the risk of historical oversimplification Janowitz examines the public school as an agent of citizenship education during two historical periods, 1890 to 1945, and 1945 to 1980. At issue in each time period is the role of the school in fostering attitudes and behaviors towards the central organs of government. In the first period, while by no means uniform or consistent, civic education was part of a search for national citizenship. Due to the flood of immigrants, schools were an instrument of acculturation, that is new values were added but the older ethnic attachments were retained. The social studies helped bridge the gap between teacher and students, between hyphenated Americans in the local communities and the larger society. History and Civics—the organization and functions of government—were taught and civic obligations were emphasized. Local community and ethnic organizations were recognized as more potent agents of citizenship education than the schools. And while ethnic relations were strained by the entrance of America into World War I, vast numbers of recent immigrants and their children demonstrated civic loyalty to the United States. Janowitz cites Pierce's (1930) study of school civic and history texts published between 1915 and 1930. She found the contents to be permeated by a patriotic spirit. "The American is taught to respect and to venerate his forebears and the institutions which they designed and developed" (p. 254).

Janowitz says that an important shift in the tone of civic education occurred during the Great Depression. "First, civic education in public school, based on a format of undeviating patriotism augmented by praise for the 'American Way,' was called into question. . . . A stream of materials involving social realism and specific social problems was introduced . . . at the high school level" (p. 98). Second, a small activist student movement arose in American colleges and high schools, foreshadowing the era of protest during the Vietnam years, arose to push an agenda of dissent from government practices that contributed to the depression. Civic education was, in effect, occurring outside of the traditional curriculum. The overwhelming majority of citizens, including students, remained patriotic. Yet, the nation was impatient with the prolonged depression, and the emphasis on traditional American virtues was met with some indifference. World War II temporarily resolved any latent discontent with the political system and any further shift in emphasis from rights to obligations.

Janowitz traces the decline in civic education to what he calls the *new communalism* that became prevalent during the 1960s and 1970s. The term represents the strong sentiments of racial and ethnic consciousness that developed in middle-class as well as economically-deprived groups. In opposition to acculturation, these groups stressed their individual identity and cultural heritage. Participation in and exposure to activist ethnic nationalism was more potent than classroom civics instruction. Student demonstrations of the 1960s and 1970s offered a form of civic education. So too did the war in Vietnam. The long-term effect has been a weakened sense of civic obligation. In fact, the newest obligation of a citizen was to criticize the political system. Watergate intensified this tendency. Rights and privileges, especially to more and better education, were stressed by minorities to the exclusion of civic obligations.

Janowitz says that the content of the civics curriculum changed beyond recognition. Civic education programs prided themselves on "myth smashing" and social criticism. Gradually, the balance between rights and obligations was lost. To make this point, he cites a study of the key elements of citizenship by Charles Merriam (1931) in which the author spoke of: "patriotism and loyalty", "obedience to the laws of society," "respect for officials and government," "recognition of the obligations of political life," "some minimum degree of self-control," "response to community in time of stress," "ordinary honesty in social relations." One would be hard pressed to find such concepts occupying a central position in the civics curriculum in schools today.

Perhaps the most serious criticism of civic education as it exists in elementary and secondary schools was made by the American Political Science Association (1971). After an extensive study of instruction in civics and government in this country this Association concluded that on the whole, it: (1) transmits a naive, unrealistic and romanticized image of political life which confuses the ideals of democracy with the realities of politics; (2) places undue stress upon historical events, legal structures and formal institutional aspects of government and fails to transmit adequate knowledge about political behaviors and processes; (3) reflects an ethnocentric preoccupation with American society and fails to transmit an adequate knowledge about the political systems of other nations; (4) fails to develop within students a capacity to think about political phenomena in conceptually sophisticated ways or a capacity to systematically analyze political decisions and values; and (5) fails to develop within students an understanding of the capacities and skills needed to participate effectively and democratically in politics. Many of these deficiencies involve the capacity to make moral judgements and understand value differences. Controversy is endemic to these situations. The civic behaviors that are most needed involve communication and consensus building on the part of citizens and political leaders.

Similarly, a study by Richard Remy (1971, p. 42) reports several problems with the scope and domain of citizenship education. These are:

1. citizenship education is often not treated as a society-wide process involving many social institutions;
2. limitations on the school's capacity to contribute to citizenship education may not be adequately accounted for;
3. citizen competence with problem-solving in the social process is frequently neglected;
4. citizenship education is not treated as a cumulative, lifelong process; and
5. the multimethod requirements of citizenship education are not fully accounted for.

A recent high school government textbook (Burns, Peltason, and Cronin 1989) addresses several of these problems in chapters on "Interests Groups: The Politics of Faction," "Movements: The Politics of Conflict," "Parties: Decline and Renewal?," and "Elections: The Democratic Struggle."

However, Pratte (1988) suggests an explanation for why the Pollyannish approach to the study of civics and citizenship described above may still pertain. He offers what he calls the "principle of vigilance." "The principle is simply that nothing that people care very strongly about can be introduced into the public schools as a topic of study unless the strongly held opinions concerning it approach unanimity. In other words, if the topic is one about which people care very deeply, and if they are divided in their deeply-held opinions, then to that extent, it cannot be introduced into public education" (1988, p. 1). Hence, civic education tends to be innocuous because both its control and substance are matters about which the public cares a great deal but remains divided.

A review of an ambitious effort in 1978 to get Congress to fund and establish a National Center for Citizen Education confirms the "principle of vigilance." The purpose of the Center was to develop citizen education curriculum material, undertake public policies studies, disseminate information on citizen education, train teachers in citizen education, and develop a national program for the advocacy of citizen education. Richard Chesteen (1982) reports that the initiative did not receive vigorous support. "Arguments made against the proposal were that the Congress would not be able to agree on the kind of 'democratic values' to be taught by the center and that by promoting citizen participation it would invoke negative images related to the earlier Community Action Programs with their direct citizen involvement which caused angry reaction from some local government leaders" (p. 21).

Application of the "principle of vigilance" to curriculum decisions in Adult Education agencies would seem to have considerable validity. Also, the principle seems to explain the intellectual contortions to sanitize and temper relationships to social change that are so prevalent in the scholarly literature. The corollary to this principle also suggested by Pratte has been equally devastating to adult civic education. Namely, anything can be introduced as a topic of study in the public schools provided it is a matter about which nobody cares a great deal or a matter which is widely believed to have no practical consequences. For Adult Education agencies this means that only noncontroversial subjects in which moral and value judgments play no role can be tolerated in the curriculum.

REFERENCES

Adams, Frank. (1975). *Unearthing Seeds of Fire: The Idea of Highlander.* Winston-Salem, John Blair Press.

American Political Science Association Committee on Pre-Collegiate Education. (1971). *Political Education in the Public Schools: The Challenge for Political Science.* Washington, D.C.

Apps, Jerold W. (1979). *Problems in Continuing Education.* New York, McGraw-Hill Book Company.

Blake, Herman. (1969). Citizen Participation, Democracy and Social Change. A Report to the Emil Schwarzhaupt Foundation, December.

Brookfield, Stephen. (1984). The contribution of Eduard Lindeman to the development of theory and philosophy in adult education. *Adult Education Quarterly, 34,* 185–196.

Brookfield, Stephen. (1986). *Understanding and Facilitating Adult Learning.* San Francisco, Jossey-Bass, Inc.

Brumbaugh, Sara B. (1946). *Democratic Experience and Education in the National League of Women Voters.* New York, Teachers College, Columbia University.

Bryson, Lyman. (1936). *Adult Education.* New York, American Book Company.

Burns, J.M., Peltason, J.W., and Cronin, T.E. (1989). *Government by the People.* Thirteenth Alternate Edition. Englewood Cliffs, Prentice Hall.

Butts, R. Freeman. (1988). *The Morality of Democratic Citizenship.* Calabasas, CA, Center for Civic Education.

Chesteen, Richard. (1982). A review of citizenship and law related education publications and organizations. *NEWS for Teachers of Political Science,* Summer, 34, 19–23.

Cunningham, Phyllis. (1988). The adult educator and social responsibility. In Brockett, Ralph G. (Editor.) *Ethical Issues in Adult Education,* New York, Teachers College Press.

Darkenwald, Gordon G. & Merriam, Sharan, B. (1982). *Adult Education: Foundations of Practice.* New York, Harper & Row.

Fletcher, Colin. (1980). The theory of community education and its relation to adult education. In Thompson, J.L. (Editor.) *Adult Education for a Change.* London, Hutchinson and Co.

Hart, Joseph, K. (1937). What price democracy?. *The Social Frontier,* 3, June.

Hirsch, Edward. (1987). *Cultural Literacy.* Boston, Houghton Mifflin.

Janowitz, Morris. (1983). *The Reconstruction of Patriotism.* Chicago, University of Chicago Press.

Jimmerson, R.M., Hastay, L.W., and Long, J.S. (1989). Public affairs education. In Merriam, Sharan B. and Cunningham, Phyllis. (Editors.) *Handbook of Adult and Continuing Education,* San Francisco, Jossey-Bass Publishers.

Langton, Kenneth and Jennings, M. Kent. (1968). Political socialization and the high school civics curriculum in the United States. *American Political Science Review,* 62, 852–867.

Lindeman, Eduard C. (1961). *The Meaning of Adult Education.* Montreal, Harvest House. (original publication, 1926).

Lovett, Thomas. (1983). *Adult Education and Community Action.* London, Croom Helm.

Merriam, Charles E. (1931). *The Making of Citizens.* Chicago, University of Chicago Press.

Mitchell, Theodore R. (1987). *Political Education in the Southern Farmers' Alliance: 1887-1900.* Madison, The University of Wisconsin Press.

Olendorf, Sandra B. (1987). Democratic Empowerment and the South Carolina Sea Island Citizenship Schools. Lexington, Western Carolina University Conference on Appalachia, ED 300190.

Oliver, Leonard. (1983). *The Art of Citizenship.* Dayton, Kettering Foundation.

Oliver, Leonard. (1987). *Study Circles.* Washington, D.C.: Seven Locks Press.

Peterson, Merrill. (1987). *The Humanities and the American Promise.* Report of the Colloquium on the Humanities and the American People. Washington, D.C., October.

Pierce, Bessie L.. (1930). *Civic Attitudes in American School Textbooks.* Chicago, University of Chicago Press.

Pratte, Richard. (1988). *The Civic Imperative.* New York, Teachers College Press, Columbia University.

Rachal, John R. (1989). The social context of adult and continuing education. In Merriam, Sharan B. and Cunningham, Phyllis M. (Editors.) *Handbook of Adult and Continuing Education.* San Francisco, Jossey-Bass, Publishers.

Remy, Richard C. (1971). *Social Studies and Citizenship Education: Elements of a Changing Relationship.* Columbus, Mershon Center, Ohio State University.

Sheats, P.H., Jayne, C.D., & Spence, R.B. (1953). *Adult Education: The Community Approach.* New York, The Dryden Press.

Stimpson, Catharine R. (1988). *The Necessities of Aunt Chloe.* Washington, D.C., Federation of State Humanities Councils.

Stubblefield, Harold W. (1988). *Towards a History of Adult Education in America.* New York, Croom Helm.

Studebaker, John. (1935). *The American Way: Democracy at Work in the Des Moines Forums.* New York, McGraw-Hill Book Company, Inc.

Thomas, J.E. & Harries-Jenkins, G. (1975). Adult education and social change. *Studies in Adult Education,* 7.

Tjerandsen, Carl. (1980). *Education for Citizenship: A Foundation's Experience.* Santa Cruz, Emil Schwarzhaupt Foundation, Inc.

Chapter 4

GOALS OF ADULT CIVIC EDUCATION

> Our public men have, besides politics, their private affairs to attend to, and our ordinary citizens, though occupied with the pursuits of industry, are still fair judges of public matters; for, unlike any other nation, regarding him who takes no part in these duties not as unambitious but as useless, we Athenians are able to judge at all events if we cannot originate, and instead of looking on discussion as a stumbling block in the way of action, we think it an indispensable preliminary to any action at all.
>
> Pericles' funeral oration
> 431 B.C.

Two questions frame discussion of the goals for adult civic education. First, "What information and knowledge, dispositions and values, and ultimately actions are required by citizens in order to attend to the public's business in the practice of democratic citizenship?" In other words, "What learning should be added to the reservoir of civic content acquired in school in order to maintain and hone the capacity for citizenship?" Second, "What conditions will best facilitate the process of adult civic education?" In one form or another these questions concerning the appropriate scope, content, and methods of civic education have engaged thoughtful minds since Pericles and Plato. The quality of democracy depends upon the degree to which civic education can assist citizens in finding meaningful bases for participation in public affairs.

The relationship is reciprocal in that civic education fosters enlightened participation and participation is its own tutor. Through participation new areas in which learning through discussion, reflection, and further study is desirable are identified. At the same time, however, participation presumes some knowledge of the community, of government, and of the problem or issue at hand. It requires skills necessary to function successfully in groups and to contribute effectively to their work. Its primary function, as Barber (1984) says, is the education of judgment which leads to rational choice. "To participate is to create a community that governs itself, and to create a self-governing community is to participate. The terms 'participate' and 'community' are aspects of one single mode of social being: citizenship" (p. 155).

Stuart Langton (1978) says that participation in civic affairs is in reality a dual movement. Both facets of it require continuing civic education. There is *citizen involvement* which is government initiated or "top-down." The intent is both to improve and to gain support for administrative decisions and government programs by including citizens on decision-making boards and committees. Much of this participation is legislatively mandated. In fact, almost all new major legislative programs at the state and federal levels contain citizen participation requirements. The second dimension of citizen participation is *citizen action.* It is a "bottom-up" effort initiated by citizens.

Learning and action are the means employed by citizens on the front end of democracy, that is, where priorities are determined and public policy is shaped. These are the means citizens employ in setting purposes for their government; in defining common interests and securing the will of fellow citizens to act. At the other end of democracy citizens learn and act in order to monitor and influence governmental officials and committees, regulatory agencies, business, industry, and voters.

Both situations noted by Langton involve learning experientially, which is consistent with the essential character of adult education. Adult civic education whose objective is informed participation has many challenges, not the least of which is that citizens seeking information and knowledge about public issues sometimes find themselves in an adversarial relationship with knowledgeable persons. Citizen involvement with the public agenda is not a behavior that is universally hailed. It is not uncommon for citizens to meet with indifference and disdain from their employees in government bureaucracies. Epistemological equality is not so much bestowed by those in possession of vital information as it is seized by citizens who recognize that without it intelligent participation is impossible. The federal Freedom of Information Act, state enacted sunshine laws, financial disclosure laws, lobbyist registration requirements, and consumer rights legislation were not measures happily adopted by those in power. Ironically, these laws themselves are testimony to the consequences of sustained efforts by citizens to study and then influence government decision-making. Democracy, at times, has been as much protective of those in power as it is participatory.

Civic knowledge, skills, and the disposition to utilize them in order to achieve a vision of the community that is desired can be furthered through purposefully structured civic education. Informed judgment and action with regard to the public's affairs—dynamic and effective citizenship in full bloom—is the goal of adult civic education. Furthermore, the goal implies that this dynamic engagement in the life of democracy is governed by civic virtue—an unselfish commitment to the common good. The rub of course, as Pratte (1988) observes is that, "Many are committed to individualism and to an individualistic logic, asserted in terms of autonomy, self-reliance, getting ahead, and keeping ahead of others regardless of the cost in human suffering; and they therefore deny the value of the public good" (p. 16). Virtue, or civic decency, that results from development of civic values consistent with life in a democratic system is an important goal in adult civic education.

As society becomes more fragmented, and conversely, the world more interdependent, and as technology improves life while making it more complex, the future of democracy will increasingly depend on the ability of citizens to make wise and unselfish choices. Machiavelli's task, to prepare one man—the Prince—for leadership, was a leadpipe cinch compared to that of insuring that a nation of citizens is sufficiently committed, informed, skillful, active, and virtuous to fulfill the office of citizen. Human nature poses obstacles to this goal in that, as Barber says (1984), "Homo politicus is dependent, yet under democracy self-determining; insufficient and ignorant, yet under democracy teachable; selfish, yet under democracy cooperative; stubborn and soliphistic, yet under democracy creative and capable of genuine self-transformation" (p. 119). At all levels—beginning in elementary school and continuing throughout life—the enhancement of the commonwealth, through the development of knowledgeable, committed, capable, and active citizens, is a continuing goal of civic education.

THE CAPACITY FOR CIVIC LEARNING

It is customary to view school and family as the major agents of civic education and adolescence as the time in which it occurs. Granted, research on learning supports the conclusion that adolescents are capable of understanding the abstractions and complexities embedded in the problems, questions, and issues that citizens must decide. Intellectual stage theorists such as Jean Piaget (1952) and Robert Kegan (1982) maintain that the capacity for formal, abstract thinking and logical deduction are the culmination of intellectual growth that occurs in the teen years.

In describing Kegan's model of intellectual development, Laurent Daloz (1986, p. 65) says that the beginning stages, "Are characterized by impulsiveness and self-centeredness; these yield to a more "other-centered" stance, in which interpersonal relationships and mutuality are paramount; this in turn gives way to the birth of a new and more separate self, from which finally evolves and "interindividual balance" in which the tension between "self" and "other" reaches a new synthesis. This emerging maturity is consistent with the requirements of citizenship in which concerns about the good of the community, what Barber (1988) calls "we" thinking rather than "I" thinking, acquire new importance.

These later intellectual stages, perhaps more pronounced during the adult years, are by definition more conceptually inclusive and discriminating. A fundamental premise of this chapter is that the adult years are a fruitful, and probably more appropriate time than adolescence for civic education to produce citizenship in full bloom. The case is best made by demonstrating the scope and complexity of challenges to citizenship in a modern democracy, including the learning required of its citizens if they are to make intelligent decisions. The problem, according to Battistoni (1985), is that civic education during adolescence fails to effectively link cognitive (intellectual and reasoning skills) with affective (emotional ties and bonds to the political community) lessons of citizenship. He concludes from his reading of the political socialization literature that neither school nor family have been able to instill political values or the necessary norms of political activity. Battistoni agrees with Richard Mereleman's (1980) observation that the civic education which is provided in formal schooling is tepid. Democratic values rarely become deeply rooted and students are reluctant to apply abstract democratic values to concrete situations of choice.

George Gazda and Associates (1980), drawing upon Piaget, explain that learning involves an interaction between assimilating new facts to old knowledge and accommodating old knowledge to new facts. While facts and knowledge are critical ingredients in civic education concerning the rapidly changing sphere of complex public affairs and problems, equally important are the values underlying different interpretations of the facts. Pollster Daniel Yankelovich (Fall 1988) claims that this democratic society is held together by a handful of core values. These values include but are not limited to: justice for all; due process of law; free expression; rule by consent of the governed; government by elected representation; government efficiency; honesty; economic freedom;

responsibility for individual actions; responsibility to others and to the community; privacy; freedom of personal association; diversity; majority rule with respect for minority rights; equal participation of all persons in government; respect for the general welfare; respect for property rights; freedom of religion; separation of powers; local control of local problems; equal opportunity; equal protection of the law; rule of law or constitutional limits on government; national security; and respect for human dignity. Fundamental disagreements arise when several of these values poignantly clash in development of solutions to resolve public issues. Adults have more experience and are better equipped to adapt to and learn from these clashes in civic values. The combination of fact, opinion, and values has special consequences when the ultimate objective is some form of action in the adult world.

Daloz (1986) explains that, "Most stage theorists focus their attention on a kind of growth that does not inevitably come with age. They are less concerned with the process of becoming older than they are with the question of growing wiser" (p. 46). It would appear that this wisdom which results from civic learning is characterized as much by unselfish dedication and willingness to act on behalf of the common good as by knowledge of facts and the intellectual acumen to understand them. The challenge for adult educators is to match the capacity that adults have to grasp the nuances, subtleties, and complexities of the problems confronting society with interest and determination to work towards their solution. It is true that adults may have no more interest than adolescents in the many issues and dilemmas associated with citizenship in a democracy, and adults also differ in ability to comprehend abstractions and to engage in deductive reasoning. Nevertheless, it stands to reason that the objectives of civic education are better attained and the significance of citizenship is more fully appreciated and understood by learners who have experienced autonomy in their lives.

Unfortunately, not all adults believe in their efficacy to judge and influence political processes. They fear that democracy has become unfriendly, even hostile, to citizen participation in public affairs. The most widely expressed sentiments are that, "You can't fight city hall" and "Politicians are all crooked." Pratte (1988, p. 94) observes that most citizens are caught between the narrowness of their everyday affairs and a vast array of local, national, and international events which bedazzle, puzzle, frighten, and mystify them. It may well be that Adult Education agencies occupy a central position for evoking and channeling citizen competence and committment to finding constructive solutions to the complex problems confronting democracy.

THE KNOWLEDGE REQUIRED OF ADULT CITIZENS

Regardless of the efficacy of school-based civic education, it is impossible to learn in advance all that will be required of adult citizens. Citizenship is an adult responsibility and requires lifelong learning to be adequately fulfilled. Fortunately, what happens in school and in the family only lays the foundation for a person's basic beliefs about freedom, equality, justice, loyalty, patriotism, and pride in nation. As Roberta Sigel (1989) says, "A foundation cannot convey a clear picture of what the finished edifice will look like. . . . We have every reason to anticipate changes in the 'building program' as the person matures. For one thing, experiences during adulthood play a crucial part in this building process precisely because adults are exposed in the course of their lives to many different and often unanticipated political experiences" (p. x). Sigel includes in her definition of political, " . . . all those activities (partisan, communal, or group) and attitudes which have the potential and/or the objective to affect the quality and character of our public lives, as well as those opinions held by private persons which governments find it prudent to heed" (p.xiv). This is especially pertinent here because it contrasts so sharply with most standard political science definitions that tend to limit the term to what government and its agencies do, how citizens react to it, and what if anything they do about it.

In adopting this lifespan development perspective to the meaning of political, Sigel departs from the mainstream of political socialization literature in which it is assumed that little change in civic learning or political orientation should be anticipated during adulthood. She develops three themes regarding civic and political learning: (1) such learning is lifelong; (2) it is highly dependent on the social setting or context in which it occurs; and (3) it is an interactive process by which persons are influenced and in turn influence their environment. Family, work, military service, natural disasters, social protest movements, and the developmental processes associated with aging all contribute to a person's view of the good citizen and sense of responsibility for maintaining the political system.

Sigel and her contributing authors do not maintain that what was learned early in life has no bearing on later orientations. Indeed, much of the foundation for civic life is in place as the young person reaches adulthood. Rather, they argue for a developmental approach that is prevalent in allied disciplines and well received in adult education literature. Only this perspective can adequately account for the growth in knowledge, skills, and commitment that adults demonstrate in promoting changes that they sometimes succeed in accomplishing in society. Individuals, says Sigel, whether adults or children—are not just passive recipients who accept whatever society and its agents ordain; they are also actors. Civic learning is an ongoing, continuous process because people are both actors and acted-upon, and they have a lifelong capacity to change.

Information, values, and action are integral elements in the learning that results from purposefully structured civic education programs that precede or supplement participation in public affairs. Each of the three elements enriches the other two as it is developed; conversely, to the extent that any of the three is not included or enhanced it diminishes the other two. Adult Education agencies that include information, values, and action in programs of civic education enable citizens to: (1) interpret existing data and collect data themselves in order to influence public decisions and policies; (2) examine their priorities and values when confronted with the challenges of an ever changing society where resources are shrinking and new technology poses both problems and opportunities; (3) acquire skills to direct social change in ways that further their vision of a better society; and (4) discover and define bases for political participation, including specific steps for practical action.

These civic competencies presume a number of basic skills, perhaps learned in school. Included are basic communication skills—reading, writing, speaking, and listening. Also necessary are intellectual skills such as the ability to process information, think critically, generate alternatives, and solve problems. Attitudes such as the disposition to work with others and the willingness to take on points of view that differ from one's own are important. And finally, civic competency rests upon a sense of efficacy—a feeling that the individual can make a difference. Many of these prerequisites may need review and strengthening in order for a citizen to participate effectively in democracy.

The textbook treatment of curriculum in adult education suggests that content is shaped by numerous factors including an assessment of need measured against standards; and that instructional methods are selected according to the objectives to be achieved. In reality, the relationship between objectives and methods in civic education is circular and spiral, governed by specific context and circumstance. For example, serving as an appointed member of a task force concerning a public reservoir could be the occasion which precipitates a citizens enrollment in a workshop on treatment and use of public water. Or, acute concern about lack of enforcement of laws governing use of a reservoir may result in formation of a property owners association to study ways in which this problem has been resolved in other localities.

The substance of adult civic education revolves around the definition, analysis, and formulation of tentative policies or solutions to societal issues that are public in nature. These areas of substance in civic education are defined in a New York State Department of Education syllabus (1987) for a high school senior government course. "A societal issue is any unresolved problem or disputed policy issue that stems from existing societal conditions, conditions that existed in the past, or conditions that may exist in the future; a policy is any rule, regulation, or law which determines how social groups will deal with societal issues; a *public issue* is one that involves a dispute between two or more interested parties (people, groups, institutions) who, either collectively or individually, consciously strive to shape public policy decisions" (p. 26). Issues do not need to be artifically constructed for purposes of an educational exercise. A partial listing of salient and perennial public problems whose resolution will occupy and directly affect society illustrates the subject matter available for adult civic education:

Family issues:
  family health insurance
  rights of children
  abuse of children and the elderly
  surrogate motherhood
  care of aging parents
  availability of day care centers
  nursing home selection
Community issues
  shelter for the homeless
  community obsenity standards
  commercial development and open space
  preservation of historic buildings
  parental responsibility for juvenile vandalism

solid waste disposal
police use of deadly force
drug trafficking
annexation and zoning
gun control ordinances

State issues

public financing of political campaigns
mental health care
jail overcrowding
capital punishment
mass transit
nursing home regulation
elder-care policies
abortion legislation
tax policies
accessibility of higher education

National issues

disarmament
most favored nation trade designations
budget deficits
immigration
spending for social programs
national defense spending
import quotas
civil rights enforcement
space exploration
constitutional amendments

Obviously, many of these problem categories overlap. All of them defy simplistic solutions. Most require citizen commitment for successful resolution. Attempts to formulate policies relative to any of these problems inevitably result in disputes.

Given the above definitions and subject matter areas it is clear that adult civic education is characterized by three conditions. First, it is context-specific. Disputes over affordable housing, taxes, economic policy, zoning, annexation; debates concerning protections afforded by the First Amendment; and the positions and philosophies of political candidates find their context in the lives of adults. The information and skills a person needs for rational participation in the discussion and in the policy-making process regarding these specific issues will vary from locale to locale but also within the same locale over time. Second, the body of civic knowledge that adults require is both continually expanding and incomplete at the same time. Uncertainty associated with the political condition as well as most of adult life is the one constant variable in civic education. Each week, if not daily, there are developments in civic affairs that challenge the capacity of citizens to respond with understanding and competence. Third, understanding of the political environment requires engagement with it. According to Comfort (Fall 1982), "As we engage in political action, we understand it better. . . . It is the individual's awareness of the limitations and possibilities of collective action which defines his/her specific responses in a given political situation. Since the conditions are dynamic, there is much we cannot know until we try it. Only in the political process are certain kinds of insights generated for citizens" (p. 15). Civic knowledge arises out of the interconnection between theory and practice.

Concerning the substance of adult civic education, Ann Maust and Lucy Knight (1978), suggest that the competencies necessary for effective participation in democracy are advanced by learning events that explore: (1) legal rights and responsibilities, and the values and principles underlying them; (2) public issues; and (3) participation for personal development and political advocacy. Participation in public projects and involvement in public problems is a living laboratory for adult civic education.

ADULT CIVIC EDUCATION AS A
REFLECTION OF DEMOCRATIC THEORY

As seen in Chapter 2, Contemporary and Classical democratic theorists differ on the questions of appropriate citizen involvement or work and appropriate citizen interactions. They hold conflicting views on the role of authority within democracy as well. It is reasonable to anticipate that these philosophical differences would be reflected in adult civic education objectives and methods.

In Classical democracy, citizenship is characterized by strong ties to public affairs and common concerns with fellow citizens. According to Battistoni (1985) in the Classical mode citizens " . . . discuss, decide, and act together to make public policy, and through such direct participation in politics, their individual character is altered, their purview is expanded, their private interest is changed into the law of the polity, and their personality is made more complete" (p. 61). Aristotle's view was that citizens take responsibility for, that is they rule over, things they have not done as well as things that they have done. He defined citizens as persons who are equal in the sense that they share in offices; they rule and are ruled in turn. Learning to be ruled is said to be part of learning to rule. The citizen contributes to the whole, to the general welfare, by participating in rule.

The ideal relationship among citizens is to have interactions among equals inhibited as little as possible by authority. Barber (Fall 1988) says that the most important interactions and conversations in a democracy are not the ones between politicians and citizens, but those carried on between citizen and citizen — lateral communication — citizens talking to one another, not being talked at or talked to by politicians and not even talking with politicians as equals. But where, Barber asks in a question that could be addressed directly to adult educators, are the institutions and agencies in this country that permit and encourage citizens first of all, before they talk to or listen to the politicians, to talk to one another?

Political scientist Richard Flathman (Summer 1981) says that Contemporary democratic theorists view this ideal version of citizenship as unachieveable and hence irrelevant in the modern nation state. They maintain that the continuous, intense and morally uplifting interactions that the ideal requires of citizens can occur, if at all, only among subgroups within the large, complex, and impersonal societies of the modern world. Attempts to achieve and sustain such interactions at the level of the political society, through adult civic education for instance, are distracting and destabilizing, encouraging the masses to meddle in matters beyond their ken. Hence, they reject both an expanded notion of citizen responsibility and education to prepare persons for it. Citizens are responsible only for what they make or choose to create — for what they have caused and certainly not for the whole. Citizenship, for proponents of Contemporary Democracy, requires minimal amounts of time, knowledge and interest — those qualities necessary in the pursuit of private gain. Since individual rights and liberties are primary, the political arena is a conduit to their pursuit. The purview of public judgment, in this view, ought to be limited. That is, keep both government and citizen concern for public well-being out of as many areas of life as possible.

Barber (1984) says that Contemporary democratic theorists promote a minimalist view of citizenship that seeks to resolve conflicts in political judgments by " . . . deferring to a representative executive elite that employs authority in pursuit of the aggregate interests of its electoral constituency" (p. 140). Citizen participation in democracy for the purpose of setting priorities and pursuing their implementation is exercised chiefly through choosing "competing elites," that is, the authorities who will represent the citizenry in the messy business of governing. In this view, provisions for civic education and the interactions over public matters that it promotes are counterculture whenever preoccupation with the personal or private aspects of life is dominant.

The question of the citizen's relationship to authority and to experts is a particularly important issue in adult civic education and in the participation in public affairs that it fosters. The arguments against active citizenship invoke subordination to authority and especially deference to subject-matter experts as an essential element in a proper moral and political order. Citizens, however, sometimes stand in opposition to the decisions and policies of authorities and to the recommendations of experts, operating as they do with differing visions of a desirable future and scrambling to learn as much as possible about the public problems, questions, or issues that are in dispute. This posture can be particularly worrisome to adult educators who may be empathetic to citizens' interest in learning but nervous about being too closely associated with the repercussions of their efforts to do so.

Flathman says that, "To be an authority is to stand in a distinctive relationship not just with a subject matter or activity but with other persons who are interested or involved in it. The latter are expected to recognize, accept, and accede to that relationship" (p. 10). He rejects a politics of authority in favor of a politics of citizenship. To be sure, citizenship presupposes authority. After all, it is an office defined by rules that are invested with authority. But the politics, and indeed the learning, that is associated with ideal citizenship contrasts sharply with a politics and an educational framework based on subservience to authority and the tyranny of experts.

Pratte (1988) says that experts fall back upon a "principle of complexity" by appealing to sophisticated knowledge as a barrier to civic competence. While it is important to have the benefit of expert knowledge in complicated policy questions, democracy is based on the premise that citizens rule. Citizens usually start with a deficit of knowledge and the challenge is to acquire relative competence. "A relativist view of competence," says Pratte, "assumes that citizens can acquire sufficient knowledge and skill to be competent in essential civic functions" (p. 159). An objective in adult civic education is to help citizens learn how to use the aid of experts and qualified professionals in making public policy decisions while limiting it to citizen review and control. The objective for citizens is to bring the knowledge and skill of experts before the high court of public good and question them as to the consequences and accountability of their judgments.

Nowhere is a politics and an understanding of citizenship based on authority more apparent than in the arena of international affairs. According to Chadwick Alger (Spring 1978), the public has been taught by professors, by the media, and by governmental officials that foreign policy is an esoteric and complex subject. Agendas are set by distant elites and answers will be provided by the President. Alger suggests that Adult Education agencies are remiss in not informing the public about their *actual* involvement in international affairs. "Omitted for the most part are the international relations of labor, of churches, of a host of fraternal, philanthropic and professional groups and of a phenomenal array of consumer, manufacturing and financial involvements. . . . We do not offer enlightenment that would make it possible for the citizen to pursue self-conscious goals through this avalanche of activity" (p. 2). As a consequence the potential for responsible participation in public affairs suggested by these involvements is diminished.

Interactions among citizens as learners are distinctive precisely because they are interactions among equals; they are interactions among persons who have no binding authority over one another in respect to the subject matters of their interactions as citizens. And it is this interaction itself, for the purpose of governing and learning, that is especially valuable. Certainly there are persons who are subject matter experts, that is, authorities who know far more about a given topic, problem, or question than the general public. But citizens must know something about the subject, problem, or question to even recognize the knowledge of the expert. And they must achieve rough epistemological parity with public officials and experts if they are to have any chance to influence decisions that are vital to their future.

This point is important in establishing some middle ground for the objectives of adult civic education between the lofty ideals of citizenship in Classical democracy and absence from involvement in public affairs that characterizes the behavior of many adult educators and other citizens who subscribe to the notion of citizenship as presented by Contemporary democratic theorists. American citizenship contains elements of both, yielding what Harvey Mansfield (Winter 1982) says is a "participatory democracy of active citizens eager for change and impatient with responsibilities" (p. 19). The problem for democracy and for adult educators is the same: how to keep citizens and learners responsible for the whole community, while leaving them free to, and indeed assisting them in reaching personal objectives. Interactions, inhibited as little as possible by authority, regarding the substantive problems of democracy with a view to initiating solutions, are important behaviors of citizenship. Therefore, fostering those interactions is an important objective of adult civic education. It is a purpose that Adult Education agencies can effectively promote.

THE SKILLS REQUIRED OF CITIZENS

The prefatory questions posed in Chapter 2 resurface here. What skills do ordinary citizens in either new or well established democracies need to have in order to be autonomous, to govern, to choose, to establish community priorities, and to direct government as the instrument of their purposes? And how are these skills acquired? Answers to these questions would seem to constitute a foundation, for example, to plans announced by President George Bush (May 13, 1990) to establish a new Citizens Democracy Corps to help the new democracies in Europe build political and legal systems to shore up their freedom by promoting free markets and the tenets of freedom.

Clearly the skills required for citizenship in full-bloom relate to acquisition of knowledge and its use in action to bring about desired social change. They are skills that warrant lifetime study and practice. Several of the skills listed in the New York State Department of Education "Participation in Government" syllabus, along with a rationale, and an explanation of enabling components will be paraphrased here to demonstrate their relevance to adult civic competence. Obviously, individuals leave formal schooling with varying degrees of proficiency in these skills and proficiency can only be maintained through use. Additionally, the group nature of much citizen learning necessitates that individuals learn group process skills and demonstrate sensitivity to interpersonal and group relations.

1. The ability to obtain, organize, and communicate accurate information regarding problems and developments that relate to the common good. *Rationale:* Citizens must deal with enormous quantities of information, some of which is highly technical. The amount of information will increase. Information from a variety of disciplinary perspectives— historical, geographic, political, social, economic, and medical—is often relevant for understanding a particular public issue and for making decisions and taking action.

   Enabling skills for getting information: these include abilities to locate sources of information; observe, listen, read, and take notes; and the temerity to ask pertinent and pointed questions;

   Enabling skills for using information: these include abilities to infer meanings, biases, assumptions, and points of view implied but not stated in a source; infer relationships such as cause and effect and time and spatial relationships among items in the data; evaluate the relevance, validity, and sufficiency of data; translate information into different media or vocabulary for communication to fellow citizens; extrapolate from the data; draw conclusions and evaluate the conclusions drawn.

   Enabling skills for expressing information and ideas: these include the abilities to present factual or objective information orally, in writing and through other media; explain different points of view or positions on a topic and present the evidence and reasoning that supports each position; disagree with a position taken by another without resorting to personal attack or denigration.

2. The ability to identify and investigate issues, generate and test hypotheses, and take and support positions persuasively. *Rationale:* the pursuit of truth is important in the life of a free society; emotion or prejudice may tempt citizens to only accept positions or conclusions that suit their purposes; the pursuit of truth, or at least accuracy, involves:

   • gathering information about the source of disagreement over an issue;

   • testing the reliability of information by checking other sources;

   • inferring relationships from the evidence that has been gathered; and,

   • translating results of the investigation into a position for action.

   Enabling skills for using information: these include the abilities to recruit interested citizens, form committees, and conduct meetings; link up with persons and agencies that can help develop strategy, raise money, write letters, and generally stimulate interest in the problem or issue; speak to community groups and build a base of support with significant persons in the community; develop educational materials such as handouts, flyers, and position papers.

3. The ability to make appropriate decisions, to identify and solve problems effectively and to initiate appropriate action.
   Rationale: Citizens in democracies make political, economic, and social decisions important to implementing their vision of a desirable future. Active involvement in democracy requires participation in discussions about community priorities and implementation of solutions to problems. Taking action involves:
   • identifying alternatives and their likely consequences for the general welfare;
   • selecting and pursuing a course of action with the best match between likely results and desired outcomes;
   • evaluating results of action, including monitoring the effects of behavior on others.

4. The ability to think critically about the assumptions, arguments, and evidence relevant to problems that concern the general welfare.
   Rationale: Citizens must evaluate words and actions of elected officials and government agents. They must compare their ideas and positions against standards of logic and some vision of the good society. They must evaluate issues and possible public policy options against the standards of their community. Citizenship does not mean blind obedience nor does it mean complying with laws and decisions only when they are agreeable. It is reasoned obedience that distinguishes the citizen from the subject. A critical and skeptical obedience is preferable to an unthinking obedience because criticism and skepticism give impetus for improvement.
   Enabling skills for critical thinking: these include the ability to articulate and engage in discussions about community standards of justice, equality, decency, compassion, and other qualities that a democracy espouses; and the ability to determine any discrepancies between the ideal and what is likely to result from actual policies and programs.

5. The ability to determine and understand citizen rights and responsibilities and how they should be exercised.
   Rationale: Democracy requires informed compliance with and, where

necessary, expression of informed disagreement with rules and laws made by elected officials.

Enabling skills for expressing dissent: these include the ability to build a base of support with like-minded community organizations; assess ones own involvement and stake in political situations, issues, decisions and policies; and strike a balance between activities intended to inform authorities and those intended to oppose and confront.

The skills of citizenship are learned through civic education programs that encourage participants to move outside the confines of what is familiar and comfortable and explore new information and perspectives. Civic education promotes the ability to make connections, to see causal situations and outcomes, and to understand the relationship between the individual and the larger community. The skills of citizenship come into play when a person sees something wrong or inadequate and joins with others to find remedies. Political empowerment, expansion of the skills of citizenship, occurs when one can talk with neighbors about an issue and act on that talk. Civic education challenges citizens to recognize the interrelationship of specific private issues with larger public problems and to use civic skills in solving them.

In short, as Suzanne Morse (1989, p. 4) succinctly states, civic competence involves:

- understanding the fundamental processes needed to maintain the appropriate interaction between government and its citizens;
- the ability of individuals and groups to talk, listen, judge, and act on issues of common concern;
- the capacity to imagine situations or problems from all perspectives and to appreciate all aspects of diversity.

The major threat to citizenship, so conceived, is the public's increasing differentiation into heterogeneous groups struggling to gain some particular advantage. According to Louise Comfort (Fall 1982), the problem is that individuals expected to be skillful in constructive and collective interaction for the common good are no longer able to identify a common basis and common goal for action. The quality of public life deteriorates as the skills of citizenship are only applied in pursuit of immediate interests within a morass of shifting government policies and vaguely defined public goals. For example, who can intelligently articulate the relationship of individual interests to public goals in the maze of welfare policies that discourage work and self-reliance, or state annexation laws that promote the interests of large land developers over those of individual property owners, or in the price support and subsidy programs that make up the federal government's agricultural policy? These are but a few examples of how specialized knowledge and special interests undermine the concept of a public agenda deserving of citizen effort and commitment.

A prevailing assumption in adult civic education is that citizens of a democracy are required to do more than pursue their private interests and advantages. There is an assumption that the creation of a republican constitutional order, and most especially, its maintenance, depends upon the acquired discipline of civic virtue and that the citizen is simultaneously thinker, actor, and moral agent. Accordingly, discussion and study of citizenship is incomplete without some discussion of the notion of civic virtue as an outcome of civic education, or, as Mary Stanley (1989) states, the expectation that, " . . . the citizen will be called upon to think well, act prudently, and judge morally throughout his or her career as a member of a democratic polity" (p. 7).

CIVIC VIRTUE AS AN OUTCOME OF ADULT CIVIC EDUCATION

The notion of promoting civic virtue through adult civic education is certainly subject to challenge. By what right and according to whose definition of virtue are these treacherous waters to be navigated? The greatest challenge to constructing educational programs in which civic virtue is an objective is the absence of universally agreed-upon standards of good citizenship. Robert Bellah and Associates (1985), for instance, found that while commitment to community still appealed to many as an ideal for citizenship, so often this value was undermined by the fierce individualism and competitiveness of modern life. They concluded that contemporary Americans had too little grounding in a common language of community and the public good.

Commenting on this fragmentation in American society Manfred Stanley (Winter 1984) observes that while citizens are described with many terms, such as consumers, producers, entrepreneurs, and entitled benefit recipients among others, these conceptions, along with loyalties of kinship, religion, ethnicity, and race, essentially divide people from one another. He complains that, "We are little disposed to think of citizens as whole persons who share an identity that is superior to whatever else divides them" (p. 7). His response to this fragmentation is to propose *deceny* as the basis for public identity. Deceny is defined as, *"compassion, wisdom, and respect for effective and fair standards of adjudication"* (p. 8). The definition suggests that a hallmark of civic virtue is moderation in the discussions and actions regarding public affairs.

David Lindberg (Spring 1983, p. 6) expresses concern that whereas citizens are expected to exercise restraint in manners and deliberations with one another, a type of "post-civil" human being is emerging who imposes his private habits of self-consideration upon his public associations. "Post-civil" individuals are characterized by an egoism manifest in the habits of acquisitiveness and envy which contributes to the extinction of civic virtue and of citizenship itself. Citizens expected to discuss and act upon public matters, do so with little temperance or moderation. Restraint and civility are qualities conspicuous by their absence in much that passes for public discourse. Manners and self-restraint are absent in most public participation in the public dialogue over issues that are emotionally charged. The intemperance which characterizes the dialogue tends to disregard the rights of others and the rules of justice.

Numerous authors lend testimony to the notion that civility and respectfulness are important components of civic virtue or decency, and should characterize participation in public discourse. For instance, Pratte (1988) defines civic virtue not primarily in terms of behavior, but rather, "It is a matter of forming a civic disposition, a willingness to act, in behalf of the public good while being attentive to and considerate of the feelings, needs, and attitudes of others. It implies an obligation or duty to be fair to others, to show kindness and tact, and to render agreeable service to the community" (p. 17). Pratte says that civic competence involves development of a civic conscience that promotes, " . . . behaving morally toward others as a response to their basic dignity and worth" (p. 166). Lindberg, drawing on the *Federalist Papers* for terminology to express the importance of civic virtue, says that democracy is always vulnerable to the erosion of the good will of "civic harmony." He suggests that over and above the natural rights of human beings, the citizen has acquired a public life of manners and habits which restrain his actions and at least partially direct them in accordance with consideration for others.

Civic education, under constitutional government, is an appropriate means to strengthen and encourage those mental habits of civic virtue. B. Frank Brown (1977) reports that the National Task Force on Citizenship Education was concerned to restore emphasis on civic virtue in the school curriculum for children by listing "to be respectful of the opinions and sincerity of others" as one of its recommended components of civic education. Similarly, civic mindedness, expressed as, "An interest in, and respect for, the values and opinions of others as they are related to societal issues" and "Respect for self, others, and property . . . " are stated as goals in the New York Department of Education syllabus for its course in government. While self-interest is usually strong, this is not necessarily synonymous with being selfish. There are connections between personal well-being and the well-being of the community as a whole.

Civic virtue includes not only decency and civility, but also paying attention to the broader common interest. At the heart of choices about concrete and specific situations lie inescapable questions about values. The choices are difficult because the values involved are often in conflict. Political choosing involves moral reasoning and acting with reference to conflicting standards about what is important to the community. The choices are usually genuine dilemmas, in that, they are never wholly satisfactory. Getting at the sources of conflict is part of the purpose of civic education. For example, should tax dollars be used to paint the barns at the county fair grounds or expand the senior citizen center? Each choice probably entails issues of equity and justice. The problem for adult civic education is to help learners develop ethical reasoning as a basis for acting when their involvement in a public issue in the first place is driven by emotional investment in a special or "hot" interest, deflecting attention from a larger view of public responsibilities.

Douglas Amy (Winter 1983) forthrightly challenges the paralysis that afflicts adult educators in the domain of morality and ethics by asserting that it is our responsibility to give citizens the analytical tools that will help them to make intelligent and moral political and policy choices. The obstacles are formidable. There is little in the current political culture that encourages concern for moral responsibility. Citizens are not encouraged to put justice or the public interest at the center of their concerns about public matters. Nor are Adult Education agencies encouraged or rewarded for forthrightly addressing the moral dimensions of public problems.

As stated previously (Boggs, 1986, p. 21–22), first and foremost, Adult Education agencies that promote civic education regarding the moral dimensions of public issues run the risk of alienating powerful persons and entities in their communities who have a stake in how the issues are resolved. It is similar to the risk confronting an investigative journalist whose reporting of a problem offends friends and allies of the newspaper editor. Knowledge and moral judgments are not neutral. Empowered through participation in adult civic education, citizens may be better prepared to approach public officials and corporate spokespersons with unwelcome questions and challenges to the wisdom of proposed solutions to public problems.

Secondly, on matters of public debate Adult Education agencies run the risk of being viewed as advocates for particular positions or for specific solutions to public problems. The role of Adult Education agencies needs to be made clear. Promoting study and reflection on public matters does not mean advocating a particular solution or point of view. Rather it means that such agencies are committed to facilitating full inquiry and understanding by the public regarding its choices. They are advocates only in the sense of helping citizens with the task of becoming informed about complex problems and choices that often have long-term consequences.

Adult civic education will inevitably prompt participants to examine the logic or rationality embedded in the moral reasoning that is being used to justify solutions and choices about public problems. Amy (Winter 1983) reviews the "good-reasons" approach to moral questions that emerged in moral philosophy during the 1950s and suggests that it is useful for this task. Moral philosophers contend that people tend to give reasons to support moral positions, and the goodness or worth of these reasons can be subjected to scrutiny. Amy maintains that for dialogue or debate about public issues to exist at all there must be some rationality to the moral judgments that are included in it. "Thus moral persuasion and discourse presuppose that morality can be debated and that moral judgments are based on reasons that can be evaluated and discussed in a rational manner" (p.4). The task in adult civic education includes helping learners to develop criteria to use in evaluating policy proposals as well as reasons given for decisions and solutions to public problems. The criteria may be strictly utilitarian, for example, choosing to do what will cause the least amount of suffering is a moral criterion. So too is cost-benefit analysis. Development of criteria for evaluating moral reasoning reduces subjectivity when judging the worth or goodness of public decisions or solutions.

Amy (p. 5) stresses, however, that the ultimate objective is to help citizens learn to be morally responsible actors. The problem is that citizens are not encouraged to put justice, or the public interest at the center of their involvement in public problems. He argues that citizens need not be morally dogmatic in order to be morally committed. So, too, Adult Education agencies can espouse a position of moral alterness without engaging in indoctrination. Amy's (p. 5) definition of indoctrination should be well understood and its practice scrupulously avoided by adult educators. It is a systematic attempt to persuade students of the validity of a belief system or position. It means (1) ruling out the possibility of accepting other positions; (2) deliberately withholding serious objections to positions or any analysis of their flaws; (3) excluding the possibility of rejecting a favored position; and (4) penalizing those who deviate from it. On the contrary, Amy argues that educators, "... must be diligent in presenting and exploring all sides of (public issues), in being open to arguments supporting other positions, and in allowing (citizens) to reasonably adopt other positions" (p. 6). Given the highly charged emotions that accompany the dialogue over most public issues, it is important that adult civic education be characterized by such intellectual integrity.

At its core, responsible citizenship involves thoughtful evaluation of and responsible involvement in public issues. Adult educators have responsibility to serve as advocates, not of specific choices or solutions to public issues, but of thoughtful and deliberate choice based on examination of what will best serve the common good. Through participation in adult civic education citizens should be able to recognize and talk openly about moral choices and to make more reflective judgments about them. Historically it has been the nature and business of Adult Education agencies to garner ideas that are relevant to human problems and to apply those ideas to the choices that have to be made. The most valuable civic education for citizens immersed in public problems is that which helps them develop criteria for judging the worth of alternative solutions and for acting responsibly. Educational institutions that relegate themselves to the sidelines in a community's struggle to determine what is right and just in the public arena miss the opportunity to provide intellectual leadership within the maelstrom of democracy.

FORMATS FOR LEADERSHIP
IN ADULT CIVIC EDUCATION

Adult civic education is a complex phenomenon that can precede, accompany, or follow participation in the dialogue over public issues and problems. The intent here is to suggest three formats for adult civic education programs, DIRECT, INDIRECT, and MEDIATED, depending on whether: (1) the information to be learned is derived from more than one academic discipline; (2) the educational program addresses specific issues or problems that affect the common good; (3) values, civic virtue and civic decency are a concern; and (4) there is an expectation of participation or involvement in civic action.

Direct Adult Civic Education

Citizens who seek education in order to participate intelligently in the discussion and resolution of specific and often emotionally charged local, national, and international issues, problems, and choices may indeed be the most aggressive and dynamic learners (Boggs, 1984). Understanding information contained in research reports and technical documents reflecting diverse disciplinary perspectives is important to their purposes. They debate the implications of what they learn from printed sources as well as from interviews with technical experts and government officials. A logical outcome of this learning effort is that citizens assume the role of educators in order to persuade neighbors and fellow citizens to adopt their point of view.

Since public issues involve uncertainty as well as conflict, the contribution that Adult Education agencies can make, while being careful to not advocate particular solutions, is to encourage the participants to think about what is in the best interests of the community. What do the facts mean and how do they fit together. What are the consequences of different choices. What values underlie the positions that are being proposed. As impartial arbiters of thorough understanding of community problems and choices Adult Education agencies are in a position to help citizens be deliberative and work through the conflicts in values that they confront in most public problems.

Developing civic education programs to address public problems and choices requires resources. Following are some criteria that may be used to determine whether civic education with an advocacy-oriented citizen group is an appropriate use of those resources. First, is the issue or problem part of a larger local, state, national, or international phenomenon? In other words, is the educational agenda truly public and capable of being expanded or generalized? Two examples can illustrate this criterion. (1) *Residents seek to influence development occurring in their community.* To speak intelligently and to be persuasive however, they need to learn that land use may be inextricably related to several factors: local regulations governing zoning, the school district tax base, a county thoroughfare plan, state law concerning annexation and impact fees, as well as water, sewer, and road infrastructure requirements dictated by regional planning review boards. (2) *Residents have reservations about a proposed toxic waste incinerator.* The civic education agenda might include several substantive topics: the national debate over toxic waste disposal, requirements of the federal clean air act, state regulations governing incinerator sitting criteria, environmental impact studies that include health hazards data, local versus state zoning ordinances, regulations governing transport of waste to be incincrated, local capacity to respond to transportation accidents, and so on. On the other hand, debate over a local gun control ordinance, or efforts to change the school calendar, or eliminate daylight savings time may offer less opportunity for developing a rich civic education agenda. Hence, the nature of the issue or choices confronting a community constitutes the first criterion.

Second, the scope or sweep of the issue or problem needs to be considered. That is, how widely and deeply does it cut in people's lives? Will inaction or pending actions or decisions affect significant numbers of citizens for years to come? How many persons and in what manner will they be affected are value judgments for which hard and fast rules cannot be written. Answering these questions will test an adult educators knowledge of the community.

Third, are the persons in a community who are questioning or seeking further information about an issue or problem reasonable and credible? It is quite common for those objecting to decisions and policies of government or corporate entities to be labeled as radicals, alarmists, ingrates, and trouble-makers. To what extent are the voices of concern representative of a cross-section of the community—of its small business owners, retirees, homeowners, housewives, young couples with families, and farmers? Again, this criterion tests the depth of an adult educators understanding of the community.

Fourth, will the community be harmed by the absence and silence of an Adult Education agency? Spokespersons for government or special interest groups present their proposals or decisions in the best possible light, sometimes accompanied by the testimony of experts, and often couched as the only available course of action in a time of crisis. On such occasions there are few forums for citizens to discuss the situation, to raise questions and to subject conclusions and value assumptions to further scrutiny. Above all, citizens are not well served by silence from the adult education community when the issues are complex and the stakes are high.

Satisfaction regarding these criteria may prompt Adult Education agencies to engage in DIRECT adult civic education by providing:

1. *Technical Assistance.* Identify and recruit resource persons from relevant disciplines with expertise and interest in the issue. Locate pertinent resource materials and extant educational programs. Identify organizations in or out of the community that have interest and competence regarding the topic. Perhaps assist in grant proposal writing to secure funding from appropriate foundations.

2. *Group Process and Maintenance.* Provide space for meetings and for storing materials. Assist with definition of problem and identification of short-term and long-range educational goals. Assist with development of a group and a committee structure that will sustain inquiry into complex questions. Perhaps assist with record keeping and budgeting.

3. *Community Education.* Assist participants in civic education activities to extend their efforts and knowledge to the wider community by: helping to design effective workshops and conferences for community education; securing space; summarizing technical information in written form for public distribution; preparing audiovisual and print materials.

Indirect Adult Civic Education

Traditional courses and lecture series formats addressing generic themes such as the workings of democratic government, the Constitution, and civism or the principles, sentiments, and virtues of good citizenship are examples. Butts (1988, p. 136) presents an educational format that pairs specific obligations of citizenship with specific rights. He painstakingly reviews relevant judicial history as well as the corruptions or distortions that have occurred in citizen behavior and societal practices. What Butts proposes to include in a high school civics program would be intellectually challenging to any audience and well worth sponsoring for adult learners. Regrettably, while the subject matter in most junior high and high school social studies and government textbooks would be enlightening, those who have already traversed this academic terrain during traditional schooling are not likely to revisit it unless there is special motivation to do so.

Such civic education initiatives are here classified as *indirect* by applying the criteria presented above for making distinctions in format. First, the subject matter to be learned is typically organized along the lines of a traditional educational course. Whereas, complex public issues do not sort themselves out according to the conventions of academic disciplines. For example, health care is a societal problem that may include information about life style, nutrition, government food subsidies, immunization programs, health insurance and national health care policy. Health care is a truly complex phenomenon and no single discipline is sufficiently comprehensive to address the many issues that it presents to citizens and policy makers. Second, traditional civic education courses have mastery of knowledge rather than choosing among alternatives or problem solving as the primary goal. Learners may incidentally apply what is being studied to specific issues in their lives as citizens. Finally, such courses usually focus on a narrow facet of politics, that is, on government and elections, and present a limited view of citizen responsibilities—such as voting, serving on juries, and obeying the law. While information is a substantive component, there is usually only tentative attention to values and a tenuous connection with involvement in public issues and problems that is necessary if citizens are to set the purposes and create legitimacy for government in a democratic society.

Of great appeal to thousands of citizens who have been exposed to civic subject matter in school are programs such as the National Issues Forums. They utilize a variety of instructional methods and devices to involve citizens in addressing special themes and problems such as national defense, national health insurance, the drug crisis, the day care dilemma, and the environment. The topics are stimulating. The resources materials are informative. The discussion process is thought provoking and the structure provides for a variety of outcomes, ranging from personal enrichment to efforts to provide direct feedback to policy makers at all levels of government. Discussion of these programs will be provided in Chapter 6.

Mediated Adult Civic Education

There is compatibility between insights that can be gleaned from the humanities or liberal arts and those required of citizens in order to solve public problems. The humanities provide a fruitful vehicle for examining the responsibilities of citizens, the perennial value dilemmas presented by public issues, and the consequences of involvement in public matters or the lack of it in both history and fiction. They provide a means, according to James Quay and James Veninga (1989, "... to see forests instead of trees, to turn information to knowledge, knowledge to wisdom" (p. 6). In fact, the original purpose of the liberal arts was to prepare persons for the role of citizen.

The humanities and citizenship form an alliance. Each presumes intellectual processes that are reinforcing. The humanities offer a *mediated* format for adult civic education in that they permit but do not require citizens to make connections between current public issues and problems and those in the past, between their lives and those who have preceded them. They can be a strong democratizing force in that they contain the insights necessary to choose wisely and to live responsibly. The connection, however, between the humanities and the challenges of citizenship is not routine. Scholars in the humanities and those in political science and social studies are prone to give each other wide berth. Yet, there is extensive overlap in their concerns, a congruence that offers great promise to revitalize adult education as force for civic improvement and social change. If, as Merrill Peterson (1987) says, a primary index of democracy's health is the vigor and quality of its public discussion and debate, then the contributions that the humanities can make to improve the quality of civic discourse and sharpen its vision of a desirable future are extremely important.

The humanities enlarge our understanding of public problems by showing us that the present generation is not the first to grapple with them and the moral dilemmas they contain. According to Lynne Cheney (1988), "The humanities provide context for the decisions we must make as a people by raising questions of social purpose: What is a just society, and how is it achieved? How do we reconcile the rights of the individual with the needs of the community?" (p. 2–3). And while millions of Americans are oblivious to the humanities, their legitimacy as traditional subject matter for adult education and their congruence with the goals of adult civic education as outlined in this chapter suggest an attractive format for adult education program development. The potential in this relationship will be explored in the next chapter.

REFERENCES

Alger, Chadwick. (1978). Local, national and global publics in the world. *International Studies Notes,* Spring, 5(1), 1–13.

Amy, Douglas. (1983). Teaching the moral analysis of policy issues. *NEWS for Teachers of Political Science,* Winter, 36, 1,4–6.

Barber, B. (1984). *Strong Democracy.* Berkeley, University of California Press.

Barber, Benjamin. (1988). Two democracies: Ours and theirs. *Kettering Review,* Fall, 32–37.

Battistoni, R. (1985). *Public Schooling and the Education of Democratic Citizens.* Jackson, MS: University Press of Mississippi.

Bellah, Robert N. and Associates. (1985). *Individualism and Commitment in American life.* Berkeley, University of California Press.

Boggs, David L. (1986). *A Dialogue of Consequence: Citizen Groups and Higher Education.* Columbus, The Ohio State University.

Boggs, David L. (1984). Citizen groups: Their significance for adult education. In Hoghielm, R. (Editor.) *Rekindling Committment in Adult Education,* Stockholm, Stockholm Institute of Education, Department of Educational Research.

Brown, B.F. (1977). *Education for Responsible Citizenship.* New York, McGraw-Hill Book Co.

Bush, George. (May 30, 1990). "Bush Plans Volunteer Corps to Assist Eastern Europe," *New York Times,* p.12K).

Cheney, Lynne. V. (1988). *Humanities in America.* Washington, D.C., National Endowment for the Humanities.

Comfort, Louise. (1982). Information, values and action in the study of politics. *NEWS for Teachers of Political Science,* Fall, 35, 1, 15–17.

Daloz, Laurent (1986). *Effective Teaching and Mentoring.* San Francisco, Jossey-Bass, Inc.

Flathman, Richard. (1981). Citizenship and authority: A chastened view of citizenship. *NEWS for Teachers of Political Science,* Summer, 30, 9–19.

Gazda, George and Associates. (Editors.) (1980). *Theories of Learning.* Itasca, IL: F.E. Peacock Publishers, Inc.

Kegan, Robert. (1982). *The Evolving Self: Problem and Process in Human Development.* Cambridge, Harvard University Press.

Langton, Stuart. (1978). *Citizen Participation in America.* Lexington, MA: D.C. Heath and Company.

Lindberg, David S. (1983). Constitutional law, liberal arts, and citizenship. *NEWS for Teachers of Political Science,* Spring, 37, 1, 6–7.

Mansfield, Harvey C. (1982). Citizenship: Ancient and modern. *NEWS for Teachers of Political Science,* Winter, 32, 19.

Maust, Ann. and Knight, Lucy. (1978). *An Analysis of the Role of the U.S. Office of*

Education and Other Selected Federal Agencies in Citizen Education. Washington, D.C.: Office of Education, ED 160 533.

Mereleman, R. (1980). Democratic politics and the culture of American education. *The American Political Science Review,* June 74, 2, 319–331 & 338–341.

Morse, Suzanne. (1989). (Editor) *Public Leadership Education.* Dayton, Kettering Foundation.

New York State Education Department. (no date). *Social Studies 12: Participation in Government.* Albany.

Peterson, M. (1987). *The Humanities and the American Promise.* Report of the Colloquium on the Humanities and the American People.

Piaget, J. (1952). *The Origins of Intelligence in Children.* New York, Norton.

Prattte, Richard. (1988). *The Civic Imperative.* New York, Teachers College Press, Columbia University.

Quay, James and Veninga, James. (1989). Making Connections: The Humanities, Culture, and Community. Racine, National Task Force on Scholarship and the Public Humanities.

Sigel, Roberta and Associates. (1989). *Political Learning in Adulthood.* Chicago, University of Chicago Press.

Stanley, Manfred. (1984). The myth of one community. *Kettering Review,* Winter, 5–10.

Stanley, Mary. (1989). Educating for citizenship. In Morse, Suzanne. (Editor.) *Public Leadership Education,* Dayton, Kettering Foundation.

Yankelovich, Daniel. (1988). Changing public values. *Kettering Review,* Fall, 40–48.

Chapter 5

CIVIC EDUCATION THROUGH THE HUMANITIES

The humanities:
philosophy, ethics, religion, history,
criticism, literature, language, linguistics,
folklife, archeology, anthropology, jurisprudence
are all about us.
They tell us about our lives, our cultures, and our societies.
They provide the traditions, interpretations, and visions
which define our existence.

Florida Endowment for the
Humanities

In this book occasional reference has been made to the importance of the humanities in adult civic education. That premise will be explored extensively in this chapter. The proposition to be considered here is that integrating the humanities in adult civic education enables the participants to acquire the information, skills and values required to understand and act upon local, national, and international public problems. Democracy benefits from informed and thoughtful civic discourse by citizens about issues of common concern. Knowledge and perspectives gleaned from the humanities act as a leaven, both promoting critical reflection and inquiry about those issues, and stimulating the social vision that leads to action.

Application of the humanities to civic life implies that the relationship between them is volatile. Each of the elements of adult civic education through the humanities that has been identified above warrants further consideration in this chapter: the humanities themselves, civic discourse, social vision, and general and specific applications of the humanities to public problems.

THE HUMANITIES

It is difficult to imagine a subject about which more has been written. Descriptions are clearly more plentiful than definitions. At great risk of oversimplification, the following brief observations provide a general orientation to the discussion that occurs throughout the chapter. These remarks also make some basic distinctions in the debate over the suitability of applying the humanities to public problems.

Charles Frankel (1981) explains the humanities this way: quite independently of any humanistic disciplines, "Human beings worship; they talk, dance, sing, paint, praise the beauties of their beloved; they tell stories, maintain legends, build monuments, try to discover facts, live by rules, make choices between better or worse, complain about injustice; they puzzle over the mysterious ways of God and man" (p. 7). In doing all these things with passion and against the backdrop of a received heritage, human beings are expressing that which is most human—values, spirit, love, imagination, and hope—the substance of life.

Naomi Collins (1989) says that in recent years the humanities councils of the states have come to describe the humanities as, "... ways of thinking about what human beings have said, done, thought, and created ... the records of human culture, connecting past to present, individuals to societies, values to actions, emotion to reason. They analyze and interpret our experience; they reflect on the human condition" (p. B-4). According to the *Report of the Commission on the Humanities* (1964), "One cannot speak of culture or history apart from them. They not only record our lives; our lives are the very substance they are made of. Their subject is every man" (p. 1). In this sense the humanities enrich individuals, communities, and nations.

In view of the creative activity of human beings, the role of humanistic scholars is to comment on and appraise this work, to establish criteria for judging its excellence and significance. According to Roderick French (1984), "Creative scholarship in the humanities offers endless *re*interpretations of some facet, some period, some artifact of that experience. Humanities scholarship ... is a continuous argument between and among the advocates of differing interpretations, sometimes irreconcilable interpretations of some dimension of human experience" (p. 51). Humanities scholars provide the background for understanding and interpreting what someone else has written, or chiseled, or sung, or in some other way produced. Their public function is not to venerate but to interpret, to find coherence, to provide a sense of continuity and direction in what others have produced, and in doing so to add to its significance for present circumstances. Eventually, beginning in the late 19th century in some cases, this thinking about human experiences, expressions, and values, past and present came to be organized into academic disciplines or fields of study such as history, literature, and anthropology.

Questions about the public dimension of the humanities, and specifically, whether and how and should the humanities be applied to public affairs elicit discussion that is strikingly similar to the discussion reviewed in previous chapters concerning the relationship between adult education and social change. Some see adult education as a matter for personal fulfillment or occupational advancement, with at most a tenuous relationship to the social order; others envision social change as an explicit purpose. Without embracing it, Bruce Sievers (1984) explains the view that the humanities, and humanities scholars in particular, are ill-suited to address public problems. Their purpose rather, is to develop minds, character, refined sensibilities, and civic virtue which only indirectly affects how people think about public issues. The primary goal of this liberal education is *paideia*, the Greek word for cultivation of educated men and women. Sievers quotes William Bennett's concern that, "Such cultivation will not occur, however, if humanities teachers and students try to turn themselves into political problem-solvers and social engineers; that is, into something they are not and were not meant to be" (p. 59). In giving major attention to the study of written texts—the best that has been thought and said—and created artifacts, humanities scholars must remain objective, free from ideological assumptions, elucidating transcendent truths, and above the fray of the public arena. According to Bennett, it is a sign of intellectual weakness to engage in mundane practical and social issues, to advocate specific or even general solutions to public problems, and a disservice to expect that the humanities be concerned with public policy.

In direct contrast, there is the tendency, again presented by Sievers, " . . . to champion an activist role for ideas which stem from the humanities—to hold that these ideas have immediate and powerful social consequences and to see the humanist's public role as elucidating those ideas and assumptions which underlie public policy" (p. 59). Not only individuals, but also communities face difficult choices that, consistent with the political condition, have no definitive answers. There are merits and values embedded on all sides of issues and limited resources is an endemic condition to their solution. Collins (1989) observes that in such situations the humanities offer a broad range of human experience. They provide, " . . . perspective, insights, and wisdom, as well as ways to approach questions through analysis and critical thinking. They can help us clarify our values and frame issues intelligently to make informed decisions and thoughtful choices. . . . They can foster an informed, thoughtful, responsible, and empathetic citizenry over its alternative, an ignorant, complacent, or bigoted one" (p. B-6). Whether informed by the humanities, or not, communities will grapple with complex issues. The humanities offer the prospect of doing so with more understanding, compassion, and intelligence.

This applied dimension, this relationship between the humanities and public problems, scholars maintain, has existed for centuries. French (1984) explains, for example, that the remarkable thing about the Renaissance, the origin of the modern humanities, " . . . was the way in which the scholarly rediscovery of the classical cultures of Greece and Rome fed into a sociopolitical critique of the culture of the day" (p. 52). He offers another example in John Locke, "whose philosophy helped to make our national rebellion legitimate in the minds of thoughtful persons." French maintains that it is humanists who have been social reformers, continuing the pursuit of justice and equality in American life while their fellow citizens in positions of influence were content with the status quo.

In advocating, or at least presenting for our consideration, alternative methods of inquiry, life-styles, and forms of social order, French says that humanists are fulfilling their duty—to stretch, clarify, and deepen our conceptions of ways of being fully human in a democracy. This is what gives the humanities, and civic education that is based on the humanities, its vitality. In introducing *A Report to the Congress of the United States on the State of the Humanities* (1985) John Ward says, "Humanistic learning is involved in those fundamental questions of what life is all about. So humanistic learning is deeply political, not political in the foolish sense that people called "humanists" have practical answers to concrete social issues, but political in the sense that humanistic learning is centered on the individual who has important questions about self and society. To learn some of the answers to those questions means the fullest and richest and most imaginative development of every single self—at least in a democratic culture" (p. xv). Civic education that presents safe, noble, and approved ideas and answers to civic problems is objective only in the sense that it represents the current consensus. Educational programs that deviate from prevailing ideology may be forerunners of a revised consensus. The characteristic approach of the humanities has always been to ask questions about everything, especially the ideas that govern our intellectual and political lives.

Again according to French, "The meaning of America" (and we might add, democracy) "has not been settled once and for all. That meaning is continuously being defined and redefined through the process of an open society. The humanities *must* be in the middle of that process. Do we want to leave the definition of America to the economists? to the engineers? to the generals? We have to be in on the argument. Not with a single voice . . . but with a chorus of voices speaking for the universality, the diversity, the dignity, the folly of human experience" (p. 54). One thing is for certain. Programs of adult civic education that apply the humanities to public problems plunge educators and learners alike into the dilemma over knowledge as virtue, and knowledge as power, over contemplation versus action, over the private and the public or social goals for which education is sought and used.

CHALLENGES TO CIVIC DISCOURSE

The culture of democracy addressed in Chapter 3 is faltering at the point of citizen participation in the dialogue over public issues. Increasing the capacity of private individuals to engage reflectively and intelligently in public dialogue is the major challenge for adult civic education. Few persons relish the prospect of expressing their views in a public forum. Even persons elected or appointed to positions of public responsibility find it difficult to express themselves clearly and distinctly. Comparison of the speeches and writings of public figures today with those of one or two hundred years ago all too clearly reveals the extent of linguistic impoverishment that has developed in the public uses of language. The extent of this decline would be even greater were it not for the services of modern professional speech writers. If the quality of written and oral public discourse among public officials who must communicate with their constituents has declined, one can only wonder how much more this facility has diminished among ordinary citizens.

There are strong pressures on civic discourse. For one, it is made more difficult by the cacophony of conflicting convictions and cultures in the national debate over issues such as economic competitiveness, the environment, deficit reduction measures, and social services; and in local debates over issues such as land use, legalized gambling, and measures to finance public transit and education. The contribution of the humanities in such contexts is not to peddle the dominant ideology in any of these debates, but as Levine and Associates (1989) say, " . . . to sensitize us to the presence of ideology in our work, and to its capacity to delude us into promoting as universal, values that in fact belong to one nation, one social class, one sect" (p. 11). In other words, the humanities can help us see ourselves and our ideologies in the context of other cultures and ideologies.

Another pressure on civic discourse is that some of the voices in the debate are difficult to tolerate. As humanities scholar Catharine Stimpson (1988) says, in a culture of democracy there are diverse voices, " . . . some dominant, some marginal, some powerful, some resistant, some submissive, some lovely, some scraping, some worthy, some scabrous. At their most harmonious, they are a collage of voices, a federation. At worst, a few are tyrannical; most muted, devious, or silent" (p. 11). A third pressure is that the agenda for discussion is constantly changing and enlarging. The civil rights movement, the women's movement, shifting demographics, the global reach and power of large and influential nations, and political and social upheavals around the world are but a few of the realities that apply new pressures on public discourse, requiring citizens to listen attentively, with intelligence, humor, and flexibility.

Philosopher Alasdair MacIntyre (1987) observes that the Vietnam War revealed a garrulous form of inarticulateness in our capacity to dialogue, "One in which we spoke at such length just because we did not know how to speak so that we could communicate across our divisions and conflicts. What was revealed then was that we were no longer able to speak intelligibly to each other on any sufficiently deep issue" (p. 18). Public opinion polls assessing the views of isolated citizens have replaced dialogue and discussion as vehicles for sharing and acquiring insights into public problems. Surface consensus masks real differences in value positions. Thoughtful preparation for discussion and the skills necessary for speaking across divisions and conflicts have declined. According to MacIntyre, "The clash of opinion is no longer understood as emerging from an historically extended argument, in which you must first immerse yourself, whose history you have first to master, if you are to have an opinion worth expressing" (p. 18). Not surprisingly, both Stimpson and MacIntyre suggest that the humanities are as essential to life in a democracy, to public discourse, as the daily realities of television, food, and sleep.

MacIntyre suggests that the skills of civic discourse can be recaptured and refined through reading and discussing common texts together — "a shared stock of texts, a shared set of points of linguistic reference, and with these to some increasing extent a shared view of what American success is and would be and what American failure is, what a hero is, what a heroine is, what the virtues and vices are" (p. 19). Charles Cole (1988), former director of the Ohio Humanities Council, reviewed several programs in which participants interacted with each other and with scholars from philosophy, music, history, cultural anthropology, literature, and comparative religion in order to address issues of public importance. The programs were presented in a variety of formats including audience discussion, bus tour, call-in radio, chautauqua, debate, exhibit with interaction, field trip, game and simulation, living history, panel presentation, town meeting, walking tour, and public archaelogy.

Whether through readings or other formats, programs of adult civic education that utilize the humanities can promote a common conversation that reinvigorates the debates of the past over public values and goals. "Among the rewards," Stimpson maintains for such efforts, "will be a far more accurate history, a far richer public culture, a far more representative public discourse, and an innoculation against the temptations of ideological simple-mindedness" (p. 12). The humanities, like the salve applied to the eyes of the biblical Tobin, have the capacity to remove ideological blinders which hinder public discourse.

ENLARGING THE SCOPE OF ADULT CIVIC EDUCATION

Presently there are three hurdles to incorporating the humanities in programs of adult civic education. They are in the form of overlapping assumptions that have contributed to the decline of the humanities in adult education generally. First is the belief that the humanities or liberal arts are primarily for purposes of personal enrichment and enlightment and lack practical application to real problems such as those posed by politics and economics. Second is the widely held impression that the humanities are an elitist luxury, — unavailable, unaffordable, and ineffective in developing behavior change. Third is the assumption that deriving insights from the humanities involves reading and mastering a rather lengthy list of classical and erudite books—a requirement that will stifle the motivation of most adults.

Apps (1979) documents the emphasis on personal enrichment to the near exclusion of other purposes in programs of adult liberal or humanities education. Most of the writing on this subject was generated by the Center for the Study of Liberal Education for Adults in the late 1950s and early 1960s (Siegle, 1958; Miller & McGuire, 1961; Knox, 1962). It is descriptive of the participants and programs developed under university and corporate sponsorship. Developing a sense of citizen involvement and responsibility in public affairs was sometimes included as an objective, but the primary concern was to help participants sharpen their creative insights, broaden perspectives, and gain appreciation of human motivation. A thematic approach, featuring rich and engaging topics—man and nature, the individual and society, literature as social and individual expression, the effects of science and technology, and nature and human values—was common.

MacIntyre (1987), on the other hand, suggests that the humanities offer insights to political or economic or legal problems. Furthermore, educational programs addressing topics such as these are impoverished when devised without recourse to the humanities. The humanities speak of community, of integrity, and of concern for the common welfare. Solutions to political, economic, and legal problems can only make sense if developed in the context of a community in which it is worthwhile to have one's political, economic, and legal interests recognized.

Unfortunately, textbooks that schematically separate adult education in the humanities or liberal arts from other supposedly more applied purposes such as social transformation or organizational effectiveness (Darkenwald and Merriam, 1980) tend to reinforce the perception that they lack relevance and applicability to organizational or public problems and policy decisions. Abraham Edel and Elizabeth Flower (1981) caution that while categorical dichotomies such as these may be conceptually useful and tidy, their power to mislead and distort is not to be underestimated. "The history of thought is strewn with dichotomies in terms of which questions were formulated, theoretical energies riveted, and answers constrained" (p. 139). The perception is widespread that the humanities neither need nor can adequately serve an external objective or purpose. Few adult educators today explicitly connect adult liberal or humanities education with the responsibilities of citizenship, and then only in the broadest of terms. Explicit appropriation of the humanities for insights to civic and community problems is uncommon. How the liberal arts or humanities can contribute to increased understanding of public issues through programs of adult civic education requires systematic study.

The criticism that the humanities are elitist in nature, not for ordinary working people, is a first cousin to the perception that the humanities are for "personal enrichment only." The basic distinction is between the *elite* and the *masses*. Edel and Flower (p. 135) define elitism as, "An outlook (including a theory) that takes this distinction to be fundamental in understanding society and culture and in guiding social policy. It takes the elite to be the source of knowledge and culture, the guardian of quality, the preserver of standards, and the proper locus of leadership and authority." They trace the concept of elitism through politics, where the task is to control the multitudes within a democratic framework; through education, where the purpose is to select from the many those who are the most able; through culture, where the creative few are identified and nurtured. "The core of elitism," they maintain, "is not the values, the excellencies desired, but the conviction that the few are the bearers of such values and that the people at large cannot participate in or create these values and perhaps not even adequately appreciate them" (p. 142). In a democratic culture, however—especially where the viewpoint of Classical Democracy prevails—humanistic learning rests on the belief that more than a select few can see and imagine and act as do the best few.

The school of Contemporary Democracy, and its views on participation of citizens in civic affairs, embodies an elitist outlook. Too much participation of the masses in government will lead to chaos. Whether in matters of land use, or taxes, or environmental policy, only leaders are able to unemotionally consider public issues and develop solutions. It is the obligation of citizens to elect their leaders and then leave decisions and policies up to them. In contrast to this elitist position, a continuous goal of the National Endowment for the Humanities and the state humanities councils has been to use what Lynne Cheney (1988) calls the "parallel schools," namely, libraries, museums, labor unions, informal community organizations, television, and radio to impart insights from the humanities to civic discourse about public problems. This practice is consistent with egalitarian ideals in adult education philosophy.

Finally, to equate education in the liberal arts or humanities with mastery of a lengthy list of great books is a truncated view of its meaning. The *Report of the Commission on the Humanities* (1964) suggests that the humanities have four components. "The humanities may be regarded as a body of knowledge and insight, as modes of expression, as a program for education, as an underlying attitude toward life" (p. 1). The body of knowledge, commonly identified with a staggering amount of reading, is a misleading way of considering the humanities. Merrill Peterson (1987) suggests that, "We regard them, rather, with certain ways of thinking—of inquiring, evaluating, judging, finding, and articulating meaning. They include the developed human talents from which texts and disciplines spring. They are, taken together, the necessary resources of a reflective approach to life" (p. 2). The *Report* (1964) says that the fine and the performing arts are modes of expressing thoughts and feelings visually, verbally, and aurally. Promoting critical ways of thinking is consistent with the methods of programs of liberal education. The attitude toward life centers on concern for individuals, communities, and the nation: for moral and aesthetic ideals, for goals, for responsible behavior, and public policies.

Peterson (p. 3–4) identifies several characteristics of the humanities that make them particularly potent in adult civic education.

First, *they have both a personal and a civic dimension.* They not only give meaning to the life of the individual, they help communities define their traditions and values; they lend substance to civic discourse.

Second, *the humanities take the long perspective.* They relate past dangers, injustices, tragedies, hopes, and fears to present ones. A trojan horse from antiquity under the guise of a gift without strings attached resembles a trojan horse today in the form of public initiatives without cost or penalty for anyone. Yet, the search for transcendent truths is misleading because, as Peterson says, "They require continual redefinition and reexamination because the old answers and the old methods may no longer serve."

Third, *the humanities represent striving for coherence and synthesis.* Myriad experts on any one problem present a babel of conflicting testimony. While final resolution and harmony among differing opinions may be an impossibility, the values embedded in various points of view can be identified and choices made.

Fourth, *the humanities may be and often are disturbers of the peace.* Their purpose is to challenge assumptions that support status quo ideology, to heighten both consciousness and expectations. As enemies of passivity and cynicism they are tailor-made for civic education that addresses public issues and seeks to bring about a vision of a better community.

Fifth, *the humanities have a moral dimension.* They foster a healthy skepticism that should be the hallmark of mature citizens and alert the learner to self-serving rhetoric and less than appropriate behavior in the realm of public affairs.

Sixth, *the humanities deal with ends as well as means.* In societies and cultures that prefer to uncouple means from ends, they focus attention on what is worthwhile and why.

Finally, *the humanities cultivate critical intelligence.* While it is not possible to derive explicit prescriptions for solving public problems from the humanities, they develop the capacity and habits of the mind that are required to evaluate and judge alternative solutions.

SOCIAL VISION CONVEYED IN THE HUMANITIES

It is common today for the general public and educators alike to question the contribution of the humanities to earning a living and coping with the pressures of life in a rapidly changing society. "Of what use are the humanities? What good do they do? Why should public money be spent to support them? In what sense can the humanities be applied to public problems?" In response, Charles Frankel (1981) suggests that the answers lie in a more fundamental line of inquiry. "What images of human possibility will American society put before its members? What standards will it suggest to them as befitting the dignity of the human spirit? What decent balance among human employments will it exhibit? Will it speak to them only of success and celebrity and the quick fix that makes them happy, or will it find a place for grace, elegance, nobility, and a sense of connection with the human adventure? What cues will be given to our citizens . . . that will indicate the values authoritative institutions of our nation . . . regard as of transcendent importance?" (p. 5). The importance of the humanities to the concerns of everyday life lies in their capacity to answer these questions.

Their connection to social vision is intimate. If social vision is society's understanding of itself and what it ought to be, the humanities are the ever-expanding repository of that self-understanding. They are the study of that which is most human. As stated in the *Report of the Commission on the Humanities* (1964), "Throughout man's conscious past they have played an essential role in forming, preserving, and transforming the social, moral, and aesthetic values of every man in every age" (p. 1). According to Robert Bellah (1989), "The humanities are concerned with the traditions and resources that help us in community or society or the life-world, to think and talk about our common moral understandings, our search for the common good" (p. 6). In this sense, the replicas of the goddess of Liberty courageously erected in Tiananmen Square and the songs the students sang to express their desire for democracy may not have been works of art, but they were certainly expressions of China's public humanities.

In creating the National Endowment for the Humanities the United States Congress emphasized the vision of a better future that education based upon the humanities can provide:

" . . . a high civilization must not limit its efforts to science and technology alone but must give full value and support to the other great branches of man's scholarly and cultural activity in order to achieve a better understanding of the past, a better analysis of the present, and a better view of the future . . . democracy demands wisdom and vision in its citizens and . . . it must therefore foster and support a form of education designed to make men masters of their technology and not its unthinking servant" (quoted in the Hastings Center publication, *On the Uses of the Humanities: Vision and Application,* 1984, p. 7). It may seem ironic that intellectual achievements of the past should be so valuable for acquiring wisdom in relation to present and future realities. According to Bellah (1985), however, "In the history of the West until quite recently the humanities were involved much more directly in social thought and action. . . . Social vision was for centuries closely linked to and largely an expression of what we now call the humanities" (p. 108). He goes on to argue that if study of the humanities offers wisdom, then application of that wisdom and social vision are intrinsic products of such study. The humanities offer a vision of a better society by holding up this culture to the image of other cultures. Bellah says, "That image allows us both to see the limitation of our own culture and to imagine other possibilities for ourselves" (p. 112). The challenge is to develop opportunities for adult civic education in which these relationships—this mediation between the humanities and the public problems facing citizens can be explored.

What militates most against appropriating the humanities in the development of solutions to public problems and in the creation of social vision is the individualist bias discussed in Chapters 1 and 2. Because of the influence of seventeenth century philosopher Thomas Hobbes, tradition as a source of wisdom and insight has fallen into disrepute. In its place, the individual, unencumbered by traditional moral, social, and political thought has become the new standard of relevance. Self-interest, usually expressed in economic terms, is preeminent. Personal experience, not tradition, is the arbiter of what is valuable. Furthermore, what is past is viewed with suspicion and perhaps hostility. What is new is chic. It is frequently observed that organizations and institutions lack memory. The past is not viewed as a resource, but rather as an impediment, something to be avoided, overcome, and abolished if possible. Modern adult education is no less Hobbesian in that curriculum is based almost exclusively on current expressions of individual interest and need. Education, recreation, and fashion alike are designed to be responsive to market demand. It is indeed unfortunate that in adult education literature marketing becomes as much ideology as instrumentality.

In summary, Bellah argues that, "The modern individualist ideologies that so dominate our consciousness...are destructive of living memory and so of social vision, for social vision cannot be manufactured on the basis of present need or feeling alone but always involves an effort to discern what is good in itself and how that might be embodied. Tradition as living memory is not . . . the mindless repetition of the past, but the creative reappropriation of the past in the context of present reality. Thus a sense of the past and a sense of the future are intrinsically related: if we destroy one we destroy the other" (p. 121). Concluding her bibliographic essay, Collins (1989) suggests that the humanities in public life represent a new frontier of culture and vision in which, " . . . humanities perspectives and approaches can be shared broadly and deeply among human beings confronted with disturbing, divisive, complex, and value-laden concerns, toward developing informed decisions and thoughtful choices in our communities, our nation, and our world" (p. C-2). It is Collins' contention that communities, poised on the brink of decisions, are better equipped to chart a course for the future and the frontiers that it holds if they engage in conversation with their social and cultural past.

GENERAL APPLICATIONS TO PUBLIC AFFAIRS

Some of the clearest thinking about the relationship between the humanities and public affairs is contained in the literature concerning the National Endowment for the Humanities and the state humanities councils whose goals include relating the humanities to the current conditions of national life. In fact, Charles Frankel (1981) says that, "Nothing has happened of greater importance in the history of American humanistic scholarship than the invitation of the government to scholars to think in a more public fashion and to think and teach with the presence of their fellow citizens in mind" (p. 15). In the initial Congressional hearings on the legislation establishing the NEH, Senator Claiborne Pell referred to the humanities as, "Those culture areas which widen the understanding of man in relation to his environment as well as to other men; man's ability to appreciate the past, to comprehend the present, to project soaring new thoughts and images, ideas, and ideals into the future . . . " (quoted in James Veninga, 1983, p. 21). It is not an exaggeration to say that the humanities are indispensable in helping citizens understand who they are as a people, where they have been and where they are going. They have the potential to elucidate current public conditions and problems, to provide fresh understanding of those conditions, their origin and development within society, and the implications of those conditions for a community's future well-being.

In recent years scholars in the humanistic disciplines have been reassessing how to bring their knowledge and perspectives to bear on public issues. According to a report of the Hastings Center (1984), "Public policy issues, scientific and technological developments, and the social role of the professions are all topics that raise questions of perennial human concern. . . . The humanities have tried to illuminate such questions by drawing on the cultural traditions of the past, by critical reflection, and by imaginative creation" (p. vi). Formerly, humanists were as unconcerned about the "applied" or "public" humanities as adult educators continue to be about liberal studies or social concerns. For most Adult Education agencies, to apply the humanities to public issues is to break new ground.

Pursuant to the purpose of applying insights from the humanities to public issues, Veninga (1983) suggests four questions that will help to clarify the task. It seems likely that consideration of these questions by adult educators, humanists, and citizens will help to clarify which aspects of the humanities, specifically which humanistic disciplines are relevant to the issues that citizens face.

First, what is the status or state of affairs that is of concern to people? The humanities can be particularly useful in understanding problems that have to do with moral, political, social, spiritual, cultural, and economic well-being. Comparisons with how a problem or issue has been addressed in other cultures and communities can be instructive.

Second, what forces, events, ideas, and processes or programs have contributed to these conditions? According to Veninga, "Every discipline of the humanities includes an historical dimension: the political theorist, the philosopher, the cultural anthropologist, the scholar of literature . . . can tell us much about those factors that have led to the current conditions of national life" (p. 24). Understanding the formative influences of an issue helps with the process of generating solutions.

Third, what are the positive and negative aspects of the issue that is of concern? There are methods of analysis utilized in the humanistic disciplines that provide for critical assessment of information, for putting problems in context, for discriminating between questions of value and questions of fact, and for determining conclusions that can be legitimately drawn.

Fourth, how does this issue or condition relate to fundamental community or national myths, ideals, and goals? Veninga maintains that it is the task of scholars in the humanities to tell us about these things; about how a nation sees itself, the way it would like to be, the things that really matter beyond the surface goals of a cable TV hook-up, a computer in every home, low interest rates, and a health club membership for every family.

The various humanistic disciplines offer different understandings of public problems. They have the potential to enrich adult civic education because they offer ways of thinking and moral insights; they suggest new ideas and present the necessary evidence for understanding the particulars of public issues. They remind us that life is multicultural and facts are elusive; and that, as Bruce Payne (1985) suggests, " . . . uncertainty and arbitrariness and subjectivity are present not only in our moral judgments, but also in our perceptions, our inferences, our frames of reference" (p. 192). A brief discussion of the contributions of philosophy and history is presented below to make this point. But a similar argument could be made for the significance of literature, folklore, ethics, anthropology and the rest of the humanities to civic education. For example, literature has always claimed to critique and mirror social reality. Kathryn Hunter (1985) says that applicability and application are traditionally the normal state of literature and literary study. Literature is able to put facts in an imaginative context, to add emotion and passion, to suggest new ideas, and to offer new ways of thinking. Through literature adult civic education programs can provide a sense of the variety, possibility, and unpredictability that surrounds public problems and their solutions.

The Hastings Center report (1984) suggests that, for a variety of reasons, *philosophy* has long been concerned with applications across the entire spectrum of micro and macro decision-making activities in society: from the most global questions of environmental and biomedical ethics, warfare, and foreign policy to decision making in business, professional practice, and personal matters. "Philosophers . . . examine the reasons and justifications for human choices . . . and explore neglected assumptions, alternatives, and options, and . . . assist in a process of justly assigning responsibility for choices that lead to human harm" (p. 16–17). Philosophy contributes standards for judging arguments about complicated issues. It insists that the value dimensions of public choices be recognized. It assists citizens in framing questions about public issues logically and carefully.

Macro decisions have to do with public policy, which Daniel Callahan (1985) defines as, "The aggregate collection of those actions undertaken by government, either by omission or commission, to advance the welfare of its citizens and the protection and advancement of its national interests" (p. 94). It is best formulated, says Callahan, by the interaction of special and general knowledge, of reason and passion, of citizens and experts who regard values as the crux of policy decisions. He maintains that when the decisions, judgments, and actions of participants in this interaction reflect the perspectives of philosophy, as well as other humanistic disciplines, they are more likely to contain, " . . . high values, display well tutored moral and historical sensibilities and vision, and advance human welfare and self-understanding" (p. 96). This is particularly important because public policies having to do with allocation of scarce resources in areas such as housing, foreign policy, or welfare are relatively impersonal, affect an indeterminant number of people, regulate large domains of human activity, and often remain in effect for long periods of time.

History is the chief subject in education for democracy and therefore in adult civic education. It has public relevance in the sense that an accurate understanding of the past provides perspectives and contexts essential to understanding choices concerning present public problems or policies. According to Diane Ravitch and Chester Finn (1987), nothing is of more importance than history, and especially constitutional history, when it comes to civic learning. "The system by which we govern ourselves today is comprehensible only if its history is understood. Otherwise it is a pastiche of seemingly random rules and capricious practices. Moreover, many of the most profound issues of contemporary society—having to do with civil and individual liberties, equality of opportunity, the tensions between freedom and order, and the relationships between majority rule and minority rights—have their origins and their defining events in the evolving drama of the Constitution" (p. 201). A sense of history is the best antidote to propagandistic slogans, knee-jerk patriotism, political posturing, censorship, and simplistic characterizations of good and evil. It promotes balanced, objective, common-sense treatment of the fundamental issues that trouble citizens in a democracy. It puts the failures and achievements of democracy over time into perspective.

In addition to philosophy, public policy, as defined above by Callahan, should also reflect a sense of history. The preparation of citizens to participate in the process of public policy analysis is an important contribution for adult civic education. This analysis function involves articulating alternatives for government to consider. It sets the stage for policymaking and is best conducted when the judgments and recommendations of citizens are informed by knowledge of history. Historical data can be used to sharpen the definition of policy problems, to aid in assessment of policy options, and to identify the constraints limiting those options. History enriches the context of decisions and helps preserve distinctive traditions. In addition adult civic education is enriched when the vehicles of public history, such as museums, historical sites, media presentations, and regional historical plays and dramatic presentations are utilized.

SPECIFIC LESSONS FROM THE HUMANITIES FOR CIVIC DISCOURSE

The Humanities and the Art of Public Discussion (1989) contains three examples of utilizing the humanities in what poet and Director of the Alaska Humanities Forum, Gary Holthaus, calls an "ongoing conversation about matters of ultimate concern." This text and the suggested supplemental readings illustrate how the humanities are resources for revisiting or perhaps being newly exposed to the traditional values that underlie civic life in a democracy, the moral and philosophical assumptions that are the framework of its civic ideals. They provide no definitive prescriptions for solution of complex public issues that require citizens to think critically and act wisely. On the contrary, their impact can be disorienting rather than comforting. Disorienting in the sense that immersion in literature and history may shatter complacency and cause assumptions to be challenged and biases to be exposed. Yet, as vehicles to stimulate reflection and enrich civic discourse each example suggests possibilities that may have been passed over and each frees the imagination to consider unconventional alternatives to public problems that are consistent with democratic ideals.

1. David J. Rothman discusses the relevance of "Confessions of an English Opium Eater," written by Thomas De Quincey and published in 1821, for the problem of drug addiction. "In the first instance, De Quincey's account makes altogether clear that addiction is not simply the response of one contemporary social class or group to one particular set of social circumstances. Drug use is so complex . . . precisely because the drugs are at once captivating and enthralling, humiliating and invigorating . . . " (p. 3). Rothman suggests that the difficulty of finding the right words to describe this problem is an indication of the difficulty of finding the right public policy. Naming the problem is hardly a neutral act. If addiction is a disease, then should resources be invested to find a cure? If a vice, then should the emphasis be on education as a means to conquer an avoidable habit? If a crime, does the answer lie with enforcing penalties? Is drug addiction a predictable response to social disorganization requiring large scale social reform? How did De Quincey overcome his addiction and what solutions are suggested by his experience? Commenting on the De Quincey narrative and its significance for public policy on drug addiction, Ann Henderson (p. 10) stresses that public policy grows out of our most deeply held values and the humanities assist citizens in getting past surface reflex responses to reveal those values.

2. The condition of family life today, when divorce and remarriage rates are high, is a subject of much concern and the focus of legislation addressing the needs of children as well as their parents. Historical "evidence" is mustered from all points of the political compass to support value assumptions expressed in legislative proposals. In "The History of Families," Joan W. Scott demonstrates that families have always been flexible and changing, with many different ways of organizing. This was true of European nobility, the gentry in colonial America, and

farming and craftsmen's families that defined family as an economic unit. "In the history of the United States, stable nuclear families have been neither a consistent ideal nor a continuous reality.... Ideals of families differ in different societies and so do the practical organizations differ from the ideals. There is no "God-given" way to organize a family; family organization depends on cultural and social practices, on legal norms, on demographic and economic conditions, and on a host of other circumstances ... " (p. 14–15).

What about the impact of women's work outside the home on their families? Are parenting and work incompatible activities for mothers? Again, Scott documents that labor force participation by married women is compatible with many kinds of family structures and with the successful raising of children. From a study conducted in 1890 she quotes what is a surprise to no one today that, "The grave drawback of much of the work done for money by married women is not that it is injurious in itself, but that it is scandalously ill-paid" (p. 18).

Commenting on the significance of Scott's study for the day care dilemma in industrialized nations Margaret Kingsland (p. 21) observes what no one wants to hear, namely, that we as a people no longer seem to like, value, or cherish children or childhood. "We undervalue those who care for and educate children. We envy those who are 'child-free.' We are reluctant to pay teachers adequately. And we often view parents who choose to stay home to rear their offspring as unserious people, at best, 'lightweights' suited for 'the mommy track' rather than the fast track; at worst, 'welfare moms' or freeloaders." Surely, the observations of philosophers, historians, literature scholars, and anthropologists are pertinent to the understanding of the public issues surrounding families and children.

3. In "Devastating Nature," historian Donald E. Worster is prompted by the Exxon *Valdez* oil tanker disaster of 1989 to examine why carelessness and irresponsibility with regard to nature have become a way of life for individuals, corporations, and governments everywhere. While not a new phenomenon, Worster observes that science has given modern people tools for unprecedented levels of environmental destruction. Furthermore, the problems are often remote and invisible, easily forgotten in the pursuit of growth and self-interest. It has also given us tools to protect and reclaim the environment, but we are reluctant to use them.

Yet, while it is convenient and satisfying in a self-righteous sort of way to blame the tanker captain or his employer for lax behavior, Worster's analysis is that a larger net is needed to capture all the guilty parties. "But who really is the victim, and who is the criminal, in a culture where endless economic growth, deregulation and free enterprise, fast automobiles, and low taxes are the slogans that get votes? Did any group—the tanker crew, the corporations, the bureaucrats, or the voting majority of citizens—really prove trustworthy? Eleven million spilled gallons suggest the answer is no" (p. 29). Pursuit of unlimited power over natural resources and the freedom they offer their possessors are the values that underlie this predicament. When it comes to the environment, power and freedom are a lethal combination. One will have to be curbed to permit full expression of the other. This is not a palatable message in societies in which greed has become virtuous.

David Tebaldi's commentary on the Worster essay underscores a lesson of history that is fundamental to adult civic education. Namely, that all decisions and actions occur in a social and cultural context that determines not only what choices are made, but also how the issues are framed and thought about. Tebaldi suggests that recent philosophical, historical, and literary studies have been spurred by a growing awareness that modern science and modern appetites are gradually and perhaps irreversibly despoiling the earth. His purpose is to underscore the role of the humanities in enlarging understanding of public issues, and offering wisdom to public-policy decisions. Citizen dialogue over the environment inevitably involves consideration of questions about values and goals that have intrinsic worth.

IMPLICATIONS FOR ADULT CIVIC EDUCATION

Given the debate concerning the relationship of the humanities to public issues, it is apparent that social vision is not necessarily a by-product of education. In this context, the ambivalence that educators have about social change as an objective of education is understandable, if not forgivable. What is needed, however, is for adult educators and humanities scholars to stand in the middle. Not in the sense of being ambiguous or uncommitted, but rather: in the middle, linking humanities disciplines and the citizens who seek to understand and influence public issues; in the middle, looking for new theories, new perspectives, new interpretations that connect the realms of literature or history, or philosophy, for example, with the things that matter to people in their capacity as citizens; in the middle, listening to citizens, hearing their questions and concerns; and in the middle, helping citizens to acquire ownership of the humanities as resources from which to draw insights and wisdom to resolve future public questions and concerns.

This middle position is not easy to occupy. It is the place where contending political factions seek to be heard. It is the place where the voices of criticism can be the most shrill. It is the place where the opportunity for misinterpretation of motives is greatest. It is the place where the chances for financial profit are small and the investment of resources necessary for education to occur is large. But it is also the place where adult educators and humanists working together can make a difference. According to Quay and Veninga (1989), "The texts of the humanities, their tradition of critical reflection and dialogue, their enduring narratives and multiple perspectives, make possible the civic conversation upon which community and culture depend. Without the connecting impulse of the humanities, the pursuit is crippled beyond repair" (p. 15). So too is civic conversation crippled unless Adult Education agencies mediate this public service scholarship in forums of civic education.

REFERENCES

A Report to The Congress of the United States on The State of the Humanities. (1985). New York, American Council of Learned Societies.

Apps, Jerold W. (1979). *Problems in Continuing Education.* New York, McGraw-Hill Book Company.

Bellah, Robert. (1985). The humanities and social vision. In Callahan, Daniel and Associates, (Editors.) *Applying the Humanities,* New York, Plenum Press.

Bellah, Robert. (1989). *The Humanities and the Survival of Community.* San Francisco, California Council for the Humanities.

Cheney, Lynne V. (1988). *Humanities in America.* Washington, D.C., National Endowment for the Humanities.

Cole, Charles C. (1988). *A Handbook on Adult Learning.* Columbus, Ohio Humanities Council.

Collins, Naomi F. (1989). *Culture's New Frontier: Staking a Common Ground.* Baltimore, Maryland Humanities Council.

Darkenwald, Gordon G. and Merriam, Sharan B. (1982). *Adult Education: Foundations of Practice.* New York, Harper & Row, Publishers.

Edel, Abraham and Flower, Elizabeth. (1981). Elitism and culture. In Agresto, John and Riesenberg, Peter. (Editors.) *The Humanist as Citizen,* Washington, D.C., National Humanities Center.

Federation of State Humanities Councils. (no date). *The Humanities and the Art of Public Discussion.* Washington, D.C.

Frankel, Charles. (1981). Why the humanities. In Agresto, John & Riesenberg, Peter.

(Editors.) *The Humanist as Citizen,* Washington, D.C., National Humanities Center.

French, Roderick. (1984). On taking sides: An academic perspective on advocacy. In French, R.S. and Moreno, J.D. (Editors.) *The Public Humanities: An Old Role in Contemporary Perspective,* Washington, D.C., George Washington University.

Hastings Center. (1984). *On the Uses of the Humanities: Vision and Application.* New York, The Hastings Center, Institute of Society, Ethics, and the Life Sciences.

Hunter, Kathryn M. (1985). Literature and medicine: Standards for applied literature. In Callahan, Daniel and Associates. (Editors.) *Applying the Humanities,* New York, Plenum Press.

Knox, Alan. (1962). *The Audience for Liberal Adult Education.* Chicago, Center for the Study of Liberal Education for Adults.

Levine, George and Associates. (1989). *Speaking for the Humanities.* Occasional Paper No. 7, New York, American Council of Learned Societies.

MacIntyre, Alasdair. (1987). *How to be a North American.* Washington, D.C., Federation of State Humanities Councils.

Miller, Harry L. and McGuire, Christine H. (1961). *Evaluating Liberal Adult Education.* Chicago, Center for the Study of Liberal Education for Adults.

Payne, Bruce L. (1985). Policy analysis and the humanities. In Callahan, Daniel and Associates. (Editors.) *Applying the Humanities,* New York, Plenum Press.

Peterson, Merrill. (1987). *The Humanities and the American Promise.* Colloquium on the Humanities and the American People.

Quay, James and Veninga, James. (1989). *Making Connections: The Humanities, Culture, and Community.* Racine, National Task Force on Scholarship and the Public Humanities.

Ravitch, Diane and Finn, Chester. (1987). *What Do Our 17-Year-Olds Know? A Report on the First National Assessment of History and Literature.* New York, Harper and Row.

Report of the Commission on the Humanities. (1964). New York, American Council of Learned Societies.

Siegel, Peter E. (1958). *New Directions in Liberal Education for Executives.* Chicago, Center for the Study of Liberal Education for Adults.

Sievers, Bruce. (1984). Introduction to the Stanford Colloquium. In French, R.S. and Moreno, J.D. (Editors.) *The Public Humanities: An Old Role in Contemporary Perspective,* Washington, D.C., George Washington University.

Stimpson, Catharine R. (1988). *The Necessities of Aunt Chloe.* Washington, D.C., Federation of State Humanities Councils.

Veninga, James. (1983). The humanities and public life: Thoughts on the work of the state humanities councils, *FR,* January/February, 20–27.

Chapter 6

SUMMARY, RESEARCH, AND RESOURCES

> We must learn, . . . to meet, as our Fathers
> did, . . . There must be discussion and debate
> in which all freely participate, . . . The whole
> purpose of democracy is that we may hold counsel with
> one another, . . . For only (then), . . . can the general interests
> of a great people be compounded into a policy suitable to all.
>
> Woodrow Wilson

In this chapter a modest sample of resources available to facilitate adult civic education is identified. Resources, in the forms of ideas and materials for educational programs, and the organizations making them available, are the staples of education. The matter of resources could well constitute an entire volume in itself. Research themes that could enrich the knowledge base of adult civic education will also be explored. To address resources and research is to move beyond exhortation and rhetoric and face temporal, personnel, and physical constraints.

The most important resources for creating forums of deliberative democracy in which citizen learners can hold counsel with one another about public problems are the educator's creativity and courage. Creativity in identifying and applying resources to educational opportunities; courage in overcoming the bias that public talk is always an adversarial expressive exercise, in the realization that public talk can be, in Jane Mansbridge's words, " . . . both raucous and constrained, conflictual and harmonious. It can turn on opinion as well as fact. It can draw on emotion as well as reason. It can help the participants think "we" instead of "I". . . . (talk) that aims at the creation of a common good" (1989). In the end, consistent and effective adult civic learning requires educational programs that promote deliberative and integrative public talk; talk that leads to public knowledge and public judgment about what is valuable for the common good; talk that leads to action to carry out the public will.

113

The following summary paragraphs draw together the theory, rationale, research, and history presented to this point that form a foundation for adult civic education. They provide context for the discussion on resources and research.

1. Adult civic education is the purposeful and systematic effort to ensure that adults have the competence and disposition to function effectively as citizens and attend to the public's business in their communities as well as in the larger world. Civic education supercedes all other priorities for adult education in free societies because a strong and active sense of citizenship is essential in a democracy. All other purposes of adult education presuppose the freedom and self-determination that democracy ensures.

2. The public's business consists of making choices and setting directions concerning those things that it shares and values in common. Public talk, civic discourse, is the vehicle for working through choices and forming judgments about public issues. Public life marks the points of interdependence among strangers who share common purposes.

3. Creating a self-governing community of citizens is made difficult by suffocating individualism that distracts people from civic responsibility and made urgent by decades of inefficacious school-based civic education.

4. The demise of totalitarian regimes in central and eastern Europe highlights the requirements of citizens to be autonomous, to choose, to establish priorities, and to direct government as the instrument of their purposes. While democracy is a hybrid of conflicting assumptions, Classical Democracy encourages citizens to both deliberate and act to bring about the public policies and programs that will best promote the common good.

5. Informed participation, that is, informed choices made after study and deliberation, is the foundation of democracy. Through the public dialogue that characterizes democracy, citizens seek to achieve rough epistemological parity with elected officials, government bureaucrats, and technical experts.

6. It is at the local level that citizens learn to govern. Local problems both affect the quality of life and engender excitement and commitment. By participating in the democratic process on the smaller scale of local problems, citizens learn how to gather information, weigh its significance, and exercise judgment and autonomy in larger national and international affairs.

7. Despite citizen requirements for information about public issues, as well as for the skills and wisdom to use it effectively, Adult Education agencies have been tentative in discharging the responsibility of education for citizenship. They have relegated themselves to the sidelines and become peripheral observers in this important sphere of life. This timidity is compounded by, and perhaps the result of, widespread disaffection with civic concerns and decline in civic literacy.

8. Particularly troublesome to adult educators is the fact that civic education in a democracy is essentially political, in the sense that learning in order to choose wisely among alternatives in public matters involves competing values and conflicting visions of the future. Furthermore, no independent standard or authority exists as a basis for deciding which choices are best. All political choices involve uncertainty and conflict.

9. Social change, predicated on an alternative vision of a community, is not easily embraced as an educational objective. In both its programs and its literature, the adult education community has been ambivalent about promoting learning in order to facilitate action to implement change.

10. Education to promote civic competence is insulated from specific problem situations. Problems as the impetus for lifelong learning are suitable grist for the mill in every facet of adult education but this one. Nor is education for civic responsibility integrated into established curriculum areas.

11. Historically, some programs of adult civic education have addressed conditions of apathy and powerlessness that are deleterious to democracy. The humanities, in the forms of song, poetry, story-telling, history, and philosophy, were often important sources of inspiration and instruction for the participants.

12. Schools have been agents of civic education. Yet, at times, participation in local community and ethnic organizations and exposure to activist ethnic nationalism were recognized as more potent agents of such education than classroom civics instruction. The "principle of vigilance," which effectively blocks substantive discussion of public issues from civics instruction for children, also seems to be operative in the adult education curriculum.

13. Informed judgment and action with regard to the public's affairs — dynamic and effective citizenship in full bloom — is the goal of adult civic education. Regrettably, curriculum decisions in Adult Education agen-

cies seem to mirror the assumptions of Contemporary Democracy theorists. That is, the dynamic context for lifelong learning which democracy presents in the form of complex decisions facing citizens is ignored. The implication, by default, is that such matters should be left to technical experts, bureaucrats, and elected officials who are assumed to possess inside and specialized information.

14. Adolescents are capable of understanding the abstractions and complexities embedded in the problems, questions, and issues that citizens must decide. Yet, the adult years, in which there is opportunity to apply abstract democratic values to concrete situations of choice, are probably a more fruitful and more appropriate time for civic education to produce mature citizenship.

15. There are three conditions associated with adult civic education: first, it is context specific; second, the body of civic knowledge that adults require is both continually expanding and incomplete at the same time; third, understanding of the political environment requires engagement with it. Information, values, and action are integral elements in the learning that results from civic education that precedes or supplements participation in public affairs.

16. Inevitably, adult civic education reflects some philosophical position on the meaning of democracy and the proper roles of citizens within it. Questions about the relationship of citizens to authority and to experts are important issues in adult civic education. Because of differing visions of desirable futures, citizens sometimes stand in opposition to the judgments of authorities and recommendations of experts. An objective in adult civic education is to help citizens learn how to both use expert advice and limit it to their review and control in making public policy decisions.

17. The skills required of citizens include the ability to: (a) obtain, organize, and communicate accurate information regarding issues related to the common good; (b) identify and investigate issues, generate and test hypotheses, and take and support positions persuasively; (c) make appropriate decisions, identify and solve problems effectively, and initiate appropriate action; (d) think critically about the assumptions, arguments, and evidence relevant to problems that concern the general welfare; and (e) determine and understand citizen rights and responsibilities and how they should be exercised.

18. Civic virtue, as an outcome of civic education, is a disposition to act in behalf of the public good while being attentive to and considerate

of the feelings, needs, and attitudes of others. It resists the erosion in civic harmony that occurs when the skills of citizenship are applied only in pursuit of private interests and when intemperate public dialogue threatens to trample on the rights of others and the rules of justice.

19. Besides decency and civility, civic virtue includes attention to the moral and ethical questions underlying public problems and choices. Citizens are required to work through the pros, cons, constraints, and consequences of various options to solving public problems. Evidence of civic virtue can be found in more open attitudes, a willingness to consider other views, movement from first opinions to more considered opinions, and appreciation of the contribution of others.

20. Through programs of civic education Adult Education agencies should advocate intellectual integrity and moral alertness, full public disclosure of information necessary to understand a public problem, and thoughtful and deliberate choice of morally defensible solutions. They may not advocate particular solutions or engage in indoctrination. Promoting civic education regarding the moral dimensions of public issues and choices is not without risk. The alternative, however, is to miss the opportunity to provide leadership within the maelstrom of democracy.

21. Distinctions in three formats for adult civic education, DIRECT, INDIRECT, and MEDIATED, are based upon criteria that ask whether: (a) the information to be learned is derived from more than one academic discipline; (b) the educational program addresses specific issues or problems; (c) values, civic virtue, and civic decency are concerns; and (d) there is an expectation of participation or involvement in civic action?

22. The humanities are ways of thinking about what human beings have said, done, thought, and created. They are records of human culture, connecting past to present, individuals to societies, values to actions, and emotion to reason. They analyze and interpret our experience and reflect on the human condition. When the humanities are integrated into programs of adult civic education the knowledge and perspectives that are gleaned act as a leaven, both promoting critical reflection and inquiry about issues of common concern, and stimulating the social vision that leads to action.

23. Considerable discussion has occurred among scholars about whether the purpose of the humanities is to develop the mind while remaining free of ideological debates and above the fray of public disputes, or to provide perspective and wisdom regarding public problems and the

ideologies behind the solutions that are proposed. These discussions are
strikingly similar to those regarding the relationship between adult
education and social change.

24. The humanities offer the prospect of helping citizens to grapple
with complex public issues more intelligently. Humanistic learning is
deeply political because it is centered on questions about the self in
relation to society. It has always been the role of the humanities to pose
questions about the ideas and assumptions that govern our intellectual
and political lives.

25. Civic discourse is debilitated by several obstacles which the humanities can help surmount. The humanities can unmask ideologies; they
can give voice to convictions and dissolve inarticulateness; they provide
context and background to issues that otherwise seem unique and
unfathomable. They disturb the peace by challenging entrenched assumptions and reinvigorate stale debates with fresh perspectives. As sources of
reflection, they speak of community, of integrity, and of concern for the
common welfare.

26. The humanities have a volatile relationship with social vision.
They offer a vision of a better society by holding up the dominant
culture to the image of other cultures. They foster imagination of other
possibilities. They challenge the individualist bias which sees self-interest
as the only standard of relevance for either education or social policy.
They restore the position of tradition and history as resources for making informed decisions and thoughtful choices.

27. Incorporating the humanities in adult civic education helps learners
to understand that public decisions and actions occur in a social and
cultural context that influences not only what choices are made, but also
how the issues are framed and thought about. Naming the problem is not
a neutral act. It conditions and predisposes citizens and policy makers to
certain solutions. The humanities, particularly philosophy, history, and
literature, free the imagination to consider unconventional alternatives
to public problems that are consistent with democratic ideals.

28. Adult Education agencies are able to link the humanities with
citizens who seek to understand and influence public issues. Adult civic
education can be designed to help citizens acquire ownership of the
humanities as sources of theories, perspectives, and interpretations regarding public business. Adult Education agencies stand in the middle,
between citizens and the public issues they seek to address. In the middle
there is the prospect of both criticism and praise, of frustration and

satisfaction, of success and failure. The humanities are excellent company when one is standing in the middle.

RESOURCES FOR ADULT CIVIC EDUCATION

The ideas, materials, and organizational models selected for discussion here have several qualities in common that add to their importance for adult civic education. First, these resources are adaptable. They can be expanded, abridged, or otherwise modified in terms of time, cost, facilities, and staff requirements to suit local circumstances. Second, local control of content, and instructional materials and methods is assumed. Third, resources in the form of educational programs that are included here model citizen behavior appropriate for a democracy. The views of experts are sought and included, but the importance of every participant's political voice, joined together in common voice, is emphasized. Participants are encouraged and expected to assume ownership for the learning process and the outcomes. Fourth, the resources are readily available. Organizations supporting adult civic education are predisposed to share ideas and materials at minimum, and in some cases, no cost. Fifth, in some instances, humanities scholars have been instrumental in shaping these ideas, materials, and program models. Finally, all three elements of effective civic education—information, values, and action—are either already included or made available by these resources.

Study Circles Resource Center

A complimentary packet of materials from the Study Circles Resource Center (SCRC) was the basis for the descriptive information that follows. In a news release dated February 1, 1990, the SCRC, located in Pomfret, Connecticut, announced the availability of services to help organizations engage learners in short highly-participatory, small-group discussions on critical local, national, and international social and political issues. By promoting study circles, discussion groups in which neighbors, co-workers, or members of an organization come together to read about and discuss issues as equals, SCRC hopes to contribute to a more enlightened, involved citizenry capable of making decisions based on informed judgment.

The study circle is small-group democracy in action. In sessions lasting approximately two hours, and directed by a prepared leader whose role is to facilitate discussion, participants discuss various controversial choices confronting society. The focus is on values that underlie opinions and almost any Adult Education agency can use this format to educate and empower its learners.

The Center operates a Clearinghouse that has a computerized data base and library that its staff can access to answer questions ranging from general inquiries on available topics to specific questions on format, point of view, and price. One-page summaries of existing topical materials are available free of charge. Some programs include recommended activities as well as materials. Available Clearinghouse topics and their contents are:

AMERICAN GOVERNMENT and SOCIETY: topics include capi—
talism, censorship, our political system, our future, and more.

ECONOMICS: this heading includes the Third World, the US farm
crisis, public debt, and the trade gap.

ETHICS, PHILOSOPHY, and RELIGION: included are such topics
as male and female roles, abortion, and racism as well as examination of how individuals can become involved in improving society.

GLOBAL SECURITY: addresses the nature of violence and war as
well as the nuclear threat and US foreign policy.

HEALTH: dilemmas and choices facing society in dealing with AIDS,
euthanasia, and health care for the elderly.

OTHER CULTURES, OTHER COUNTRIES: emphasis is on learning about other societies and people with different backgrounds,
and appropriate US foreign policy toward them.

SCIENCE and the ENVIRONMENT: this heading includes the environmental crisis, science and religion, and genetic engineering.

SOCIAL PROBLEMS & POLICY: a variety of problems are examined including crime, drug abuse, and poverty.

Of course, it is not possible to have, in advance, suitable material for every public issue that may arise. So SCRC has prepared a 32-page publication, *Guidelines for Developing Study Circle Course Material,* to assist organizations with the task of producing homemade materials. The *Guidelines* address pragmatic concerns such as clarifying goals, developing a time frame, segmenting and sequencing the content, and incorporating ancillary print, audio, and film materials. Combinations of homemade and Clearinghouse materials are common.

As adult educators are well aware, a successful program hinges on more than the materials. A careful plan, with responsibilities of various participants clearly spelled out, is essential. The 32-page, *Guidelines for Organizing and Leading a Study Circle,* stresses that there is no one program plan nor one right way of organizing adult civic education. Each sponsoring organization and leader should create and shape the program to suit its own circumstances and the needs of its constituents. Discussion as a method of learning is promoted according to the best adult education tradition, and the process—democratic discussion among equals—models the behavior expected of citizens. One page summaries of the guidelines described above are available free of charge.

SCRC has developed special clusters of activity to promote civic education in churches and labor unions. Its ideas and materials have been adopted by several organizations. It is aggressively pursuing opportunities to be of service to others. Founded in 1988 as a nonprofit, nonadvocacy program, SCRC brought the study circle model back to America from Sweden, where it had been adopted as an adult education concept that was pioneered in the 1870s by the Chautauqua Circle. It is dedicated to strengthening democracy by increasing the participation of a concerned, informed public.

National Issues Forums

The 1990–1991 National Issues Forums (NIF) Leadership Handbook and interviews with staff of their founding organization, the Kettering Foundation, were sources for the descriptive information presented below. In addition, materials that describe adaptations of NIF to suit local needs were obtained from selected partners among the 1,700 civic and educational organizations using the NIF method. The overarching research question which the Kettering Foundation attempts to be instrumental in answering through its NIF programs is, "How does the public learn the public's business?" The forums, often designed according to a study circle model, provide citizens an opportunity to study and dialogue regarding public issues, to consider a broad range of policy choices, and to identify the concerns they have in common.

Each year since its inception in 1982, through a participatory process involving its network members, NIF identifies three issues for public discussion and then develops and distributes background information in the form of nonpartisan issue books (information). In addition to the issue books, a humanities perspective is provided by the Education

Branch, Office of Public Programs of the National Archives in supplementary historical documents about the issue. They are the raw materials that researchers use to write history but do not require training as an historian to be useful. Discussion questions relating to the historical documents are included. Examples of issues chosen for citizen dialogue in recent years are: The Day Care Dilemma, The Drug Crisis, The Environment at Risk, Coping with AIDS, Health Care for the Elderly, The Public Debt, Freedom of Speech, Crime, The Farm Crisis, Regaining the Competitive Edge, and Growing Up at Risk.

Next, in local forums and study circles citizens work through an issue by discussing societal choices inherent in it, weighing the pros and cons associated with various choices, analyzing alternative solutions, and searching for commonalities (values). The historical documents may be used by a moderator to initiate discussion or establish historical perspective or challenge the basis for strongly held opinions. It is in making choices that values become apparent. The initial choices presented for the issue, Growing Up at Risk, were:

1. Teaching values: at the root of young people's tragedies is their inability to distinguish right from wrong. We need to teach them values so that they will make the best decisions for their futures.

2. Restoring order: children and teens need a safe environment in order to grow and flourish. Our first priority should be to discipline the troublemakers in order to give other young people a chance to prosper.

3. Providing care: we have people who know how to treat the problems of young people. All that our experts need is the time and money to give it a fair shot.

4. Building futures: we need to attack the problems of youth at the roots. Young people will continue to get into trouble as long as they grow up impoverished, with poor educations, and deprived of a community.

Finally, after discussion of these choices and adding more of their own, participants search for vehicles by which their views, informed by information, can be conveyed to decision-makers and have an impact on the policy making process (action). The NIF forums do not set out to directly affect public policy or to push it in a specific direction. Action outcomes are indeterminate and variable. For some, the personal development that results from being involved in the process is sufficient reward in itself for participating. Others find an application of what is learned in shared conversations with neighbors. Some initiate action in the workplace. Others make contact with policymakers individually or in groups. On occasion, policymakers are invited to come and listen. The variety of ways to influence the policymaking process is limited only by the energy and imagination of participants.

Support in the form of resources is available from NIF in the form of guidelines for choosing a steering committee, moderator guidelines, suggestions for designing the forums, recommendations on promotion and recruitment of participants. Ultimately however, the program is controlled, supported, and developed by sponsoring agencies in local communities who are interested in a form of adult civic education that allows participants to: develop public knowledge and public judgment, find common ground, develop standards for directing and evaluating their government, and along the way, become citizens in a fully functioning sense. Adult educators in these agencies believe that citizens have a stake in public policy, in the way that policymakers think and act on public issues, and in the way decisions are made in the policy arena. Examples of NIF partners who organize and conduct forums or study circles are churches/synagogues, county cooperative extension agencies, libraries, municipal leadership groups, senior citizen centers, community colleges, community groups, prisons, and a few continuing education facilities.

Brief explanations of adaptations of NIF forums that three different sponsors have made to suit their individual circumstances are included to illustrate the concept of local control. These programs reflect their coordinators dedication to adult civic education and willingness to promote it over and above other responsibilities.

The Indianapolis Program for Literacy and Citizenship

Funded by a grant from the Lilly Endowment, the Indianapolis Program is a three-year project of the Indianapolis Adult Literacy Coalition. It uses the National Issues Forums process and materials to introduce a civic component into adult literacy programs. It seeks to include the Coalition's target populations, people who are often left out—people with little education, those who cannot read well, people who are unemployed or poor, young adult dropouts, and low-income minorities—in discussions of important issues that affect all citizens. As a means of taking part in public life and giving direction on important issues to local, state, and national policymakers, the program helps participants to come to know and understand each other and their community. It also seeks to improve the written and verbal communication skills of the learners, to increase their self-esteem, and to connect them to the community in ways that they are not usually connected. Other organizations involved in teaching basic skills to adults, such as social service agencies, neighborhood centers, and community organizations concerned with minorities and the disadvantaged have also been included.

Corrections Education

Over 90 percent of incarcerated persons are released back into society and expected to function as citizens. Because inmates easily lose touch with the values systems of free society, and because their interpersonal and reading skills are often deficient, the issues addressed in NIF materials and programs take unique shape when adopted in prison settings. The issues are pertinent to successful adjustment because, while inmates may have heard about what is going on in the outside world, they lack a sense of belonging to it. The coordinators report that several objectives are being addressed at once. For instance, male and female inmates in two South Carolina prisons discussed "The Day Care Dilemma" together. All were enrolled in school and had children, and all took the issue of child care seriously. They helped each other with interpreting the reading material and were respectful to one another. Women appreciated hearing a male point of view. Natural leadership emerged in the discussion groups. The program was a positive literacy tool.

At Clallam Bay Corrections Center in Washington State inmates tackled the problem of crime from the victim's point of view. The program is limited in 5-week segments because of frequent changes in the prison population. Reading and writing skills are expected along with oral communication. Various literacy levels are accommodated. Exposure to different ways of thinking permits change in attitudes.

At Westville Correctional Center in Indiana, adult basic education students have been able to participate in discussions of NIF materials with inmates enrolled in college classes. Participants choose the topics and meet for five–six weeks in hour-long study circles that culminate in panel discussions with all participants present and leaders from the surrounding community invited to respond and give insight on the issue under discussion. Organizers of the program have learned not to underestimate the abilities of those with less education. Participants have discovered some resident experts whose lives have been directly affected by particular issues under discussion. The forums have been videotaped and aired to the general public on a local cable television station. The local newspaper ran feature stories on the program, giving its readers a perspective on the value dimensions of issues that they would not otherwise have had.

National Issues Forums in the Catholic Community

The United States Catholic Conference (USCC), in conjunction with NIF, has prepared a leadership handbook that adapts the NIF process to the Catholic tradition. The intent is to complement what already exists by adding its own tradition of Catholic teaching on social issues and a spiritually enriching component of prayer and celebration. In the Catholic tradition adult civic education is a vehicle to explore the moral dimension of public choices, the possibility of either enhancing human dignity or eroding it by public policies.

The handbook suggests additional materials pertaining to a given issue from Sacred Scripture and portions of papal encyclicals and documents issued by the USCC to be included with those from NIF. The NIF process has also been modified to incorporate a shared practices methodology that encourages learners to share experiences through the use of worksheets followed by discussion. The premise is that precisely because the moral content of public choice is so central, the religious communities are inevitably drawn more deeply into the public life of the nation. From its inception in 1988, when the program was piloted in eleven locations, the program has grown many times over and is hosted now in parishes, campus ministries, neighborhood centers, and ecumenical settings as well.

No doubt other religious traditions have developed and implemented educational programs on civic issues. The churches and synagogues have a long history of involvement with social issues such as hunger, homelessness, immigration policy, world peace, and many others.

The State Humanities Councils

Under the auspices of the National Endowment for the Humanities, the state humanities councils have become leaders, forging links with many organizations, but especially, the educational community, to enrich the knowledge and perspectives of citizens. Since the early 1970s, either on their own, or through collaboration with other agencies, the state councils have developed lectures, seminars, and exhibits on themes that demonstrate the value of the humanities to civic life and are central to the civic education of citizens. In addition, at least 38 councils have created resource centers containing films, books, artifacts, posters, and other resources that are routinely made available to support civic education. The resources for this purpose that are developed by the separate state councils are described in *Be Resourceful,* a quarterly newsletter that is currently edited by Brian Crockett (1990) and sponsored by the Federation of State Humanities Councils.

While a thorough accounting of state humanities council accomplishments remains to be written, Esther Mackintosh (1987) and Wilson Grabel (1990) have written profiles of sample programs for the Federation of State Humanities Councils. Four examples are included here to suggest the potential that they offer for adaptations by Adult Education agencies.

1. Absorption of immigrants into its public life is a problem that confronts all democracies. For example, the school board, teachers, and citizens supporting the public schools in San Francisco need to be knowledgeable about the cultural differences of a student population that speaks at least 30 languages. The California Council for the Humanities spearheaded a program to help teachers deal with this cultural diversity and promoted development of curriculum materials on new immigrant populations. This information would be instructive to a broad range of audiences that seek to be better informed about the many public issues surrounding immigration.

2. The Virginia Foundation for the Humanities and Public Policy developed three programs that brought humanities scholars together with diverse segments of the public to consider three highly charged issues: "Coal: Its Environment, Its Future"; "Intelligence and Testing"; and "Genetic Engineering." The issues associated with these complex technical themes sharply divide citizens and yet understanding the human side of the controversies in all three issues through history and ethics was most essential to achieving understanding, resolution, and progress. These programs illustrate the value of keeping the humanities central to discussions of even the most technologically sophisticated problems facing citizens today.

3. In West Virginia, the humanities council published a statewide newsletter, established a speakers bureau, and held a statewide teleconference — all to celebrate the Bicentennial of the United States Constitution. The spin-off possibilities in terms of themes for civic education were limitless.

For example, seminars on First Amendment issues alone could not exhaust the choices citizens confront in issues such as pornography, flag burning, freedom of the press, and separation of church and state.

4. In Washington, D.C. there is a palpable craving among the District's 65,000 public housing residents for programs that will boost literacy and encourage personal self-development. "City Lights," a program of reading, film-viewing, and discussion was the catalyst for engaging residents in lively discussions about their past, their community, and their neighbors. It has prompted residents to design their own humanities programs that will focus specifically on literacy.

Upstream/Downstream: The Humanities and the Environment (1989) is a project of the Ohio Humanities Council and the George Gund Foundation that has diverse components that lend themselves to adaptation for adult civic education. Twelve posters illustrating environmental choices facing Ohio, particularly in the use of its five major rivers, have been the impetus for reading and discussion programs offered primarily through public libraries throughout the state. Background information in the form of essays by three Ohio scholars in philosophy, literature, and history and a list of recommended readings were developed for use in seminars. With the help of a humanities scholar at each location who served as a catalyst for discussion, participants used the posters, essays, and supplementary reading to gain understanding first, about current attitudes toward the environment and the use of natural resources, and second, appreciation that Ohio's environment is a product of many individual and corporate choices.

The text of the introductory poster succinctly frames the issues and the value of the "Upstream/Downstream" analogy to citizen dialogue over difficult environmental choices.

> "All (five major rivers) begin their courses as clean water. But far upstream they start to pick up impurities, which they carry downstream. Soon they are only as clean as the environment and people along their banks. What is put into them affects life downstream.
>
> Our ancestors changed Ohio in their attempts to "tame" the land. What they did affects us today. In a sense, we live downstream from these earlier settlers. Choices we now make about our water, land, and air will affect those who come later on the river of time. Actions taken here may affect people elsewhere in the state and beyond.
>
> The terms "upstream" and "downstream" emphasize how people influence one another in their use of natural resources. Rivers are symbols of these connections, linking people, communities, and environments.

Studies of other cultures and societies have shown us that not everyone relates to the environment in the same way. Not every culture would have made the same choices which our ancestors made in bending nature to human purposes. . . . " (1989)

The last poster in *Upstream/Downstream*, "A Time for Choices," states several questions appropriate in discussions about acid rain, the greenhouse effect, deposits on bottles and cans, water supply, development in the face of destruction of natural habitats, critical resource areas, and national energy policy to reduce dependence on foreign oil, to mention just some of the issues that confront citizens in the search for what constitutes the common good.

"Can we learn from previous generations and set a balanced course?
Can we learn to share responsibility for our common resources?
Should we develop a new way of thinking about nature that is based on a broader sense of people's needs?
Must we learn new habits so that we don't live well at the expense of others 'downstream'?
Is it time to recognize the interdependence of all living things?"

Available for purchase from the Pennsylvania Humanities Council is a twelve-panel poster exhibit, *To Preserve These Rights* (1990), to explore the history and contemporary significance of the Bill of Rights. Each panel engages viewers with vivid graphics, photographs, and quotations by statesmen and jurists. It is accompanied by an 80-page *Users Guide* featuring essays, a bibliography, a filmography, and suggestions for educators. Other state councils are using this exhibit to encourage proposals for public programs and discussion groups that focus on the fundamental importance of our Constitutional system and the rights and responsibilities implied by citizenship.

Examples of resource materials for traditional courses on government, the Constitution, Law, Authority, Privacy, Justice, and Responsibility — labeled in Chapter 4 as INDIRECT ADULT CIVIC EDUCATION — are contained in the Catalogue of the Center for Civic Education (1988). While these materials are directed to youngsters in grades K–12, they are readily adaptable to adults whose reading skills are at comparable levels. A recent publication by Suzanne W. Morse (1990), *Renewing Civic Capacity: Preparing College Students for Service and Citizenship*, provides several recommendations for developing citizenship awareness on college campuses where increasing numbers of adults can be found.

There are also three publications that consistently furnish timely and provocative information that is relevant to adult civic education. *The Civic Arts Review* (1988–), published by the Arneson Institute at Ohio Wesleyan University, is dedicated to presenting ideas and practices that illustrate the relationship between the liberal arts and good citizenship. The *Kettering Review,* published by the Charles F. Kettering Foundation, presents articles that are concerned with improving the quality of life in the American democracy. The Council for the Advancement of Citizenship promotes citizenship education through a variety of vehicles, including its CIVITAS mini-grants that support civic education initiatives in schools and community settings. The Council publishes *Citizenship Education News,* a newsletter that contains information about recent publications on civic education and news about its activities.

The imperative for adult civic education is fed by an inexhaustible list of public issues. Opportunities for adult educators to collaborate with state humanities councils and other organizations such as those described in this chapter in order to expand the pool of resources for adult civic education are ample. The task is made more difficult, however, by lack of confidence on the part of educators in the capacity of citizens to resolve public problems, and by the view that democracy is no more than an adversarial system in which conflicting interests attempt to win some advantage. Neither tendency is particularly creative or courageous.

THEMES FOR RESEARCH IN ADULT CIVIC EDUCATION

The knowledge base for adult civic education might resemble what has been developed for other facets of the adult education enterprise. However, the lack of attention in the professional literature to the specifics of adult civic education is indicative of a scarcity of distinct civic education initiatives on the part of Adult Education agencies. Important clusters of research questions concerning who participates and why, what learning occurs, how does learning impact civic behavior, what forces shape curriculum, and what program planning models are used have not been extensively addressed because of minimum investment in civic education.

Until this situation changes a more fruitful line of inquiry would be to examine the extent to which civic knowledge, skills, and attitudes have been incorporated as a part of other adult education programs. Is there evidence of intent to include civic content in adult basic education, for example? Does continuing professional education concern itself with the civic responsibilities of participants? In either case, how is civic content expressed? What learning outcomes are expected? Is the amount of emphasis similar for different categories of learners: prisoners, dentists, welfare mothers, public officials, for example? What proportion of rights versus responsibilities is emphasized? What is learned and what was intended? The focus of such research could be on isolated programs or an aggregate of them in some manageable fashion.

In those instances where Adult Education agencies have collaborated with organizations whose announced purpose is to promote civic learning, research on the nature of those relationships may be instructive. For example, what is the nature of political fallout for Adult Education agencies that invest resources in civic education? What is their response to it? What is the role of public policymakers in such programs? How readable and unbiased are the instructional materials? What orientation is provided for discussion leaders? How is controversy managed? How does the experience vary for private versus public Adult Education agencies?

Obviously there is potential in adult civic education for developing a rich and complex research agenda whose fertility stems in no small measure from being so directly related to issues of vital concern to citizens. In Chapter One the question raised was: "What might citizens of western Democracies tell residents of central and eastern Europe about what it takes to maintain a democracy?" The question might well be turned around and directed inwardly because in Eastern Europe, while people were still subjected to totalitarian regimes, there emerged what Vladimir Tismaneanu (1990) refers to as, a civil society.

According to Tismaneanu, the civil society refers to the voluntary association of individuals committed to social change and to a politics of the people rather than party labels and ideologies. It exists outside the orbit of government to promote dialogue about what kind of society is desirable and action to make it possible. It includes membership in unions, professional associations, and religious institutions; the human rights, ecological, and pacifist movements; and other groups committed to rescuing the individual from the all-embracing official ideology. Through membership in such organizations people learned not to entrust government with sole responsibility for determining what is good, not to fear participation in dialogue over issues of public importance, and not to fear criticism and the risks of divisiveness.

Since belonging to such organizations took moral courage, perhaps the truly important research questions are those prompted by Tismaneanu's essay. Namely: How did leaders in those countries, many of whom were primarily concerned with the education of adults, who were perhaps already in jail, or whose activities were carefully monitored, manage to persuade people to engage in prolonged discussions about the kind of society that they would give their lives to create? How did they convince a depoliticized populace of the advantages of engaging in politics—a populace that was dominated by authoritarian paternalistic governments and treated as infants incapable of governing themselves? And finally, of the people themselves, what is to be learned from their rediscovery of individual rights, the separation of powers, accountability of elected officials, legal guarantees for exercise of constitutional rights, and the dignity of truth?

Furthermore, at a time when curriculum in Adult Education agencies reflects the dominant position of science and technology in society, as well as an overriding preoccupation with employment and productivity, a second cluster of overarching research questions has to do with the significance of the humanities to civic discourse. "How can the practical and public purpose of the humanities be demonstrated? How to demonstrate, in the words of John Churchill (1985), that they have more than decorative value, a trivial though elegant luxury for the leisured?" In the public dialogue over abortion, AIDS, the environment, the deficit, freedom of speech, drugs, intervention in foreign affairs, and other thorny problems it is important to identify how the humanities help adults to arrive at clarity on questions such as: "What is truth? What is a theory? What is science? What is a fact? What is scientific evidence? What is intellectual honesty? What is civic virtue? What constitutes freedom, and what is coercion? Where is pluralism permissable, and what does justice demand that the state protect?"

These and other research questions raised above underscore the significance of adult civic education. To the extent that it is subsidiary to other educational purposes, citizens are diminished and Adult Education agencies are relegated to the sidelines in this most important sphere of life in a free society. To the extent that it is enlarged and made prominent, the promise that adult education holds for strengthening democracy, promoting social action, and encouraging critical discourse on public issues is revived.

REFERENCES

Center for Civic Education. (1988). *Center for Civic Education Catalogue.* 5146 Douglas Fir Road, Calabasas, CA 91302 Phone (818) 340-9320.

Churchill, John. (1985). The humanities in public conversation. *Midwest Quarterly,* Winter, 238–248.

Civic Arts Review. The Arneson Institute, Ohio Wesleyan University, Delaware, OH 43015.

Council for the Advancement of Citizenship. 1724 Massachusetts Avenue, NW, Suite 300, Washington, D.C. Phone (202) 857-0580.

Crockett, Brian. (1990). (Editor.) *Be Resourceful.* Quarterly Newsletter of State Humanities Resource Centers. Utah Humanities Resource Center, 340 East 100 South, Suite 100, Salt Lake City, UT 84111 Phone (801) 359-9670.

Federation of State Humanities Councils. 1012 Fourteenth Street N.W. Suite 1207, Washington, D.C. 20005 Phone (202) 393-5400.

Grabil, Wilson. (1990). *Explorations in the Humanities: Projects Nominated for the 1989 Schwartz Prize.* Washington, D.C., Federation of State Humanities Councils.

Indianapolis Program for Literacy and Citizenship. 1500 N. Delaware, Indianapolis, IN 46202, Phone (317) 638-1500.

Kettering Foundation. (1990–1991). *National Issues Forums Leadership Handbook.* National Issues Forums 100 Commons Road, Dayton, OH 45459-2777, Phone 1-800-433-7834. In Ohio: 1-800-433-4819.

Kettering Review. Charles F. Kettering Foundation. 200 Commons Road, Dayton, OH 45459-2799.

Mackintosh, Esther. (1988). *Explorations in the Humanities.* Washington, D.C., Federation of State Humanities Councils.

Mansbridge, Jane. (1990). Hard decisions. *Report from the Institute for Philosophy and Public Policy,* Winter, 2–4.

Morse, Suzanne. (1990). *Renewing Civic Capacity: Preparing College Students for Service and Citizenship.* Report No. 8, ASHE–ERIC Higher Education Report, The George Washington University, One Dupont Circle, Suite 630, Washington, D.C. 20036.

National Issues Corrections Forum. *CORRECTIONS 1990.* Dayton, NIF.

National Issues Forums. (no date). *National Issues in the Catholic Community.* Dayton.

Ohio Humanities Council. (1989). *Upstream/Downstream: The Humanities and The Environment.* 695 Bryden Rd. P.O. Box 06354, Columbus, OH 43206.

Pennsylvania Humanities Council. (1990). *To Preserve These Rights.* 320 Walnut St., Suite 305, Philadelphia, PA 19106, Phone (215) 925-1005.

Study Circle Resource Center. (1990). NEWS RELEASE. Route 169 P.O. Box 203 Pomfret, Connecticut 06258, Phone (203) 928-2616 FAX(203) 928-3713.

Tismaneanu, Vladimir. (1990). Eastern Europe: The story the media missed. *The Bulletin of the Atomic Scientists,* March, 17–21.

AUTHOR INDEX

133

SUBJECT INDEX